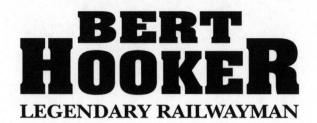

BERT HOOKER

LEGENDARY RAILWAYMAN

BERT HOOKER

LEGENDARY RAILWAYMAN

A. E. Hooker

Oxford Publishing Co.

A catalogue record for this book is available from the British Library.

ISBN 0 86093 447 0

Oxford Publishing Co.
is an imprint of Haynes Publishing,
Sparkford, near Yeovil, Somerset, BA22 7JJ

Printed in Great Britain by
Butler & Tanner Ltd, Frome and London.

Typeset in Times Roman Medium by
Character Graphics (Taunton) Ltd.

Contents

Foreword

by R. H. N. Hardy

BERT HOOKER IS a good friend; as steadfast as they come. We have had some grand times together and it has always been a pleasure to arrange a new experience for him to add to his vast store of knowledge of railways and railwaymen. When we meet, it is I who do the prompting, and he the talking for he is vastly entertaining and interesting, particularly about the people with whom he worked. They were mostly strangers to me, for Nine Elms was Sou'West and Stewarts Lane truly a Chatham shed and the men were as different as chalk and cheese. So we never worked at the same shed which enabled us to become close friends in a way that would have been impossible for either of us, had I been in charge at Nine Elms instead of Stewarts Lane. Now we are bound closely by our love of railway work as it was in the hard but magical days of steam when comradeship, skill and morale, punctuality and discipline were of the utmost importance.

Bert, like the legendary Sammy Gingell of Stewarts Lane, is a gentleman in the true sense. He is natural with people in all walks of life and with those in authority, without losing an equally natural and friendly dignity. He commanded universal respect both as a fireman and as a driver and yet he never chose to become a foreman or footplate inspector. The many compromises which had to be part of the foreman's life were alien to Bert's nature and to practise them would have worried him, so he wisely remained a driver, where he was happiest, up to his retirement.

Bert differed from old Sam in many ways but particularly in appearance when on the footplate. Whereas Bert was meticulously clean and smart, Sam was black within the hour and gloried in it but what a man he was, the strongest of the strong. And when he was fighting the cancer that eventually killed him, it was Bert, the man who had never worked with Sam except when 'off duty', who visited him in his last years to talk about the job they both loved and of the men who made the railway what it was.

When I was Divisional Manager at King's Cross and the pressures were fairly intense, I would take a day's fresh air and exercise with Bert. We would share the work and I would be back in the office refreshed and invigorated. On two occasions we took French *mécaniciens* with us,

6

old friends of ours, and what marvellous days they had dealing with the Bulleids on the Bournemouth road when Bert's supervision would be constant but his interference rare. My Calais friends never forget to ask after "Bébert" nor do I forget the retirement party that we held for the Calais Chef Mécanicien, Edmond Godry, at BRHQ in the Senior Officers' Mess. We were well turned out for it was a unique occasion, but Bert stole the show when he arrived, immaculate and in his smartest driver's uniform and highly polished shoes. Proudly, he wore his long service ASLEF badge for he was a good trade unionist and a man of strong principles. He had been a prominent Branch official at Nine Elms and no doubt, he wrote many a letter in his beautiful copperplate hand.

If Bert has a weakness, it is his fondness for vinegar. How he loves the stuff! We were in France together and had spent the night at the Abbeville dormitory. We had No. G81, a PLM Pacific with Henri Dutertre and Little Louis, his gigantic fireman. We worked the 0600 to Amiens, turned and returned to Calais with Train 9, the morning boat train. Our trip was improved, if this were possible, by the appearance of a bottle of good red wine, served with great care by that distinguished connoisseur, M. Dutertre, while I fired to Bébert up the long hill out of Boulogne. Later, we went to Henri's home in Bleriot Plage and settled down to a perfect meal, cooked and served to perfection: succulent underdone roast beef with garlic and dressed salad, fit to make the mouth water. No English spoken nor understood of course, a brief silence and then in Bébert's inimitable and confident Cockney voice: "Richit, will you ask Henri if they've got any vinegar". Not even for you, Bébert, would I make that request, fit for a Bateman cartoon!

At home everywhere and never more so than with our friend Reginald Jennings, who had been a famous Housemaster at Marlborough College. He had always wanted to travel on a steam locomotive and it was nearly too late. Reginald's world was very different to ours and it was essential to find the right man to host him on the footplate. I knew it would work with Bert but I never dreamed that the two men from such different backgrounds would be sitting side by side in the messroom at Bournemouth, eating sandwiches, within a couple of hours of meeting. What is more, calling each other by their Christian names, for this was 1966 when the immediate and mutual use of the first name was a rarity. On the way back to London, on No. 73037, Bert whispered in my ear: "Richit, shall we let Reginald have a little drive up the bank?" What joy my photograph revealed on the features of the Marlborough man as, for the only time in his life, he drove that old engine steadily up from Hinton Admiral and what serenity and strength of character was reflected in the face of the Nine Elms' man standing watchfully behind him. A scene I shall never forget. But there you have it. Bert is a perfectionist, not only in his own work and life but in the art of consideration and of giving pleasure and happiness to others. Albert Edward Hooker, Engineman, I salute you!

Preface

BERT HOOKER JOINED the Southern Railway's Locomotive Running Department in May 1934. The Management had 'put around' that any drivers who had sons aged between sixteen and twenty years and who, providing the medical examination was passed, would like to become engine cleaners should apply. His father was a motorman at Dartford on the South Eastern Section of the Southern, where he had worked since 1906 when it was part of the SECR, and up to 1926, entirely steam operated. Naturally, Fred Hooker (known as "Old 90" amongst railway men) would have liked his son Albert to have joined either at Hither Green Depot (newly opened) or his last steam shed, Bricklayers Arms. However those depots had their allocations of new entrants filled, (six to each depot in the London area) and so the aspiring footplateman was sent to New Cross Gate, thus breaking any continuity of divisional working the senior Hooker may have envisaged. But now it was the Southern and the Central Section was tolerable as Bert's cousin, Fireman Ern King, had transferred to Newhaven from Slade Green when that depot was turned over to electric traction in 1926.

Young Bert spent almost six happy years at New Cross Gate, cleaning the engines of Billintons, Marsh and Maunsell, and learning the rudiments of firing and boiler management during the 626 firing turns worked during that period. He attended the Mutual Improvement Class, administered by Driver 'Sam' Bucknole who had begun his career at Nine Elms in 1908. He intrigued the young man with his tales of big engines, the 'King Arthurs', etc., and when a vacancy sheet was posted in early 1940 advertising firing jobs at Nine Elms Depot Bert applied for one successfully, along with Arthur Jupp who later became a footplate inspector on the way to becoming Depot 'Guvnor' at Waterloo in the seventies. Sam assured young Hooker that he would do well at the Premier Depot, and so it proved.

When Fred Hooker was informed that Albert was going to Nine Elms his response was laconic, "He'll soon know what real work is like." Firing duties during the 'blackout' and the Blitz on London produced their hectic times but progress through the links was fairly rapid and main line firing was soon enjoyed, despite the ravages of war. With the war over in 1945 the depot and men adjusted to peace time, and in late 1946 the Top Link saw Bert firing on MN No. 21C20 *Bibby Line* to Driver Bill Edmonds. Bert passed the examination to act as a driver in February 1947 but the culmination of his firing career was to be selected to fire to Jack Swain in the 1948 Locomotive Exchanges on Mr Bulleid's Pacifics, as told previously. This now takes the story on to the driving days on the Southern Region of the then new BR and through to the new traction and retirement.

1

Early Driving

MY MAIN LINE firing now appeared to be finished as, following the 1948 Locomotive Exchanges, in which our Pacifics had caused a few eyebrows to rise, the Nine Elms roster clerk Fred Wild had indicated to me that as from Monday 19th July, I would be booked out driving and he could not see me going back to firing. So on this date I signed on duty at 1.45pm as a driver, although still a 'passed fireman', on a menial job 'under the hopper'. This involved placing the loaded coal wagons, one at a time on to the hoist, where it was securely clamped into position, then hoisted up to the hopper summit where the wagon was turned over, its load of coal falling directly into the massive bunker, which held up to 400 tons. Prior to being hoisted the trucks were placed under sprinklers to help lay the inevitable dust. There was but one man in charge of these operations and it devolved upon him to ensure the bunker was sufficiently filled with coal to last for at least 16 hours. It would have been somewhat disastrous to run out of coal during the 'small hours' when outgoing engines required to be topped up, as replenishing the hopper would not occur until about 7.30am.

Another event frowned upon by local authority was 'allowing' a wagon to follow its load of coal into the bunker, as it was somewhat difficult to get a crane up there to lift it out! Therefore checking the security of a truck on the electric hoist was a 'must'. 'Under the hopper' was the province of green carded drivers, usually men failing in health or eyesight but who could adequately perform on 'light work'. Two drivers and two turns, were involved; the 6.15am man prepared the engine and took her off the shed at 7am, sometimes placing an empty wagon in the wood choppers to be loaded up with split, outworn sleepers for the use of the steamraisers. This was done on the way to the adjacent loco sidings where the loaded coal wagons, which had arrived during the night were picked up. These would be shunted out, dust dampened down and several loads of coal deposited in the bunker to ensure that a good supply of nobbly coal was available for the engines working the Bournemouth and Salisbury services from 8.30am onwards.

During the morning Bournemouth and Salisbury crews would arrive and they liked to refill their tenders with good hard coal for their return journey, sometimes giving the coalmen the 'price of a pint' when the coal ran well and lumpy. The early turn man also made up a train of empty coal wagons (ironclads) to take over to Nine Elms Goods, often struggling to get out of the shed precincts on its rising gradient on track which was not exactly maintained to main line standards! The engine, usually an Adams G6 Class 0-6-0T, would return with a string of loaded coal, descending into the Loco Yard with due care and attention to prevent it getting out of control and causing possible mayhem. After this the early turn men were relieved by the afternoon shift men who completed the necessary shunting etc. The engine was then despatched to the shed around 5.30pm and was 'put away' ie., smokebox, fire and ashpan cleaned and it was then left in the care of the steamraisers. The Running Shift Foreman usually found another job; dispose and prepare an engine in order to avoid showing too much 'standing spare' on the driver's ticket (a daily record of the work done). Because of the truly menial nature of the turn the fireman booked on the job was, inevitably given to the most recent lads to be booked out firing – really ideal work on which a chap would learn to 'find his feet'.

So, on my first occasion on the turn I had a cleaner on his first firing turn, both of us feeling our way in somewhat alien worlds. Not for me the glamour of a main line turn so early in my driving career, as had happened on very rare occasions to some of my colleagues. During the Second World War several men had been engaged for cleaning engines and firing on shunting duties only, they having been deemed unfit for the armed services, but were directed to the essential jobs in the engine sheds 'for the duration'. One such man, I think he was named Len Harvey (not the boxer) lingered on for some time after the war, working in the depot but, to his regret, not on footplate work, even of the menial variety. 'Under the hopper' had been his habitat until the essential works order was rescinded and footplate work was fully restored to men 'in line of promotion'.

Nine Elms Goods Yard

Within a week or so, sometime in August 1948, I was rostered as a driver on Nine Elms Goods Yard. By this time all the engines had been fitted with a vacuum brake and no longer was it necessary to call out 'Woa!' to the fireman when one needed to stop – a vast improvement in working conditions. My first regular fireman was a very tall young man named Jim Marsh, who had a real interest in the job and I was able to teach him the rudiments of footplate work as far as was possible on a G6 shunting tank engine. Jim subsequently went through the links at Nine Elms and was with Tom Smaldon in No. 1, but because of impending dieselisation, he left the service. He figured prominently in Colonel H. C. B. Roger's book *Steam from Waterloo* (David & Charles 1985) writing therein of his recollections.

All the old 'green carded' drivers who were on the yard at the time I was firing had now long since retired and in their place were other drivers who had failed in health etc., and were committed to 'light duties'. Also of course, there were other chaps of a similar seniority to myself who were also rostered. During this period, the 350hp diesel shunters began to appear and we had just a couple of days' instruction by a footplate inspector and were then deemed qualified to drive the new machines. At first it was quite novel to be able to do the job in comfort, a seat to sit upon, the reversing lever six inches long instead of four feet, the latter requiring real physical effort to go from 'fore gear' to 'back gear', but most important of all, we were single-manned.

The depot itself suffered a gradual loss of work, and consequently there was a continual tightening up of the roster so that the number of men shown thereon was being nibbled away at quite regular intervals. The war had long since been over, with its attendant necessary work making for larger links and rapid promotion, but now this tendency was reversed. During the 1948 Interchange Trials, Dan Knight had indicated to me that Firing Instructors were to become part of the Fireman Training Scheme. Because of the quick turnover of firemen young cleaners were booked out firing before they were really ready for it, and to alleviate this position somewhat, instruction was to be given, especially in the classrooms. The theoretical side of firing and locomotive boiler management would be dealt with, along with an inkling of the rules and regulations. Danny had hinted that I would be considered favourably if I applied for this type of work. Whilst I was in the Top Link as a fireman on No. 21C20 *Bibby Line* I had taken charge of three or four cleaners and shown them the rudiments of footplate work; handling fireirons, cleaning smokeboxes, and raking out ashpans, along with the filling of hydrostatic lubricators and trimming of headlamps etc. All this was part of their footplate education and foretold the coming of Firing Instructors.

Running Shift Foreman?
However, one of the running shift foremen (R/F) approached me one day and suggested I might apply for a vacancy on the running shift foreman's panel, whereby after the three-week learning period one would be expected to shoulder the mantel of the R/F. At a depot like Nine Elms this was a job not to be undertaken lightly. I did apply for the vacancy and got it, going through the period of learning the duties of the foreman. Upon reflection one should have been put through a 'men management' training course at the same time!

There were two such men on each shift at the depot at the time – the R/F himself and his outdoor counterpart who supervised the movement of engines in the Loco Yard, and who saw that they came out of the shed ready to take water and coal, ready for the road, in their proper sequence. That job entailed more problems and heartburn than was at first realised. Some drivers were not ready to move when wanted, whilst others were only too ready and willing to get away, even before their booked time! On one occasion I saw Mr R. Steele, our Motive Power Officer at Woking, to ask if there was a possibility of becoming a future Footplate Inspector. He answered, "every chance, but first you must 'come out' as a temporary firing instructor." I was instructed to join George Bollen, the existing instructor, for a couple of weeks, to go around with him to the various depots and to get to know his routine. Monday was spent at Nine Elms, Tuesday at Feltham, Wednesday saw me at Guildford, Thursday at Basingstoke and Friday at Reading. At each of these depots all the available cleaners, having just started on the job, were booked in to see the firing instructor on their allotted days, the mutual improvement classroom at each place being used for the indoor instruction. After two weeks of my own introduction to the work, I took on the job of teaching the youngsters, whilst George was elevated to footplate inspector. I was given a footplate pass which indicated that I could ride on the footplate giving instruction if and when necessary. George had given me copies of the rules which he taught to the cleaners, consisting chiefly the duties of trainmen when detained at signals, protection of the opposite and adjacent running lines during accidents or breakdowns, protection of the line in the rear, and dividing the train if the engine was unable to take the whole of the train forward. It was all part of an educational plan in which I would have revelled, had I been given such an opportunity to learn when I first joined as an engine cleaner at New Cross Gate in 1934.

I liked the job best of all on summer Saturdays when I was booked to be on hand at Nine Elms to give any assistance as may be required. If a young cleaner was called upon to work a main line train then I was expected to go with him and show him how it should be done. So I often did a spell of firing and enjoyed it, once again adding strength to my theory that firing locomotives was more interesting than driving them! One thing I found strangely irksome during the seven or eight months I did this job, was going to work around eight o'clock every morning with a short day on Saturday, plus Sundays off. When not required at Nine Elms on Saturdays I had to go to the MP Officer's domain at Woking to complete a report on my work of the week. I must confess that I did not really enjoy the continuous classroom work, and when I received a letter at the end of the summer service, indicating that I would be returned to Nine Elms for the winter to resume driving duties I was not too sorry. Whilst I was there I came in for the occasional R/F duties, and one thing I disliked intensely about being 'on the panel' was that one was expected to do a 12-hour stint 'at the drop of a hat'. Another thing which I found somewhat distasteful was when drivers, whom I had formerly respected as good trade unionists, would approach me and ask for overtime! At this time the sand boxes on the Bulleid Pacifics were filled on disposal duties and the time so spent was booked in addition to the normal disposal allowance time, so that even if the sand boxes only required to be 'topped up' a man would book an hour doing so. One senior driver was really 'put out' because I did not condone this work on overtime. "How can I allow you to book overtime when I've got spare men in the cabin?" I asked him, "I can give that work to one of those chaps; it will show something on his ticket." I found that the job on the management side of the Locomotive Running Dept., was not all honey; often it was a case of 'running with the hare and riding with the hounds' and after giving the matter a great deal of thought I resigned from the R/F's panel. The lure of the footplate was too strong, and as a driver I would be my own 'guvnor' when away from the depot.

Other duties which befell a spare man on the panel was the covering of the M.P. Supervisor in Clapham Yard (day work only) and Waterloo (early and late turns) whose small office was situated at the country end of No. 11 platform which, in later years, became the focal point for loco spotters. One small item which hastened my decision was that on the retirement of Mr J. P. Maitland as Running Shed Superintendent, his successor, Mr Smith, was merely designated as Shed Master, which I felt was the beginning of the end of the old Southern Locomotive Running Department.

The Dual Panel
During the time I was on Nine Elms Goods Yard several vacancies appeared on the Dual Panel. This was a number of drivers and passed firemen who were trained on electric traction, learning the necessary roads which included all local lines out of Waterloo, Reading, Alton and Portsmouth. I made an application to join the Panel as I felt that with the knowledge of these lines I would be able to work steam trains as and when necessary in addition to working electrics.

On the first of April 1949, exactly nine years after I was appointed a fireman, I gained the coveted title of Driver, and coincidentally my three-week training period on electric traction commenced. Drivers from other depots were on the course also, I think the total was six, and we were required to report to our instructor in his 'office' at the top end of London Bridge No. 7 platform. He was a former guard on the Central Section. Known as the 'half-a-crown' men, there were certain guards that were given basic training on motormens' driving duties so that if a motorman was taken ill whilst out on the road the guard could come up to the front cab and drive the train to the next station, or wherever another driver could be obtained. For this emergency knowledge the guards were paid an extra 2s 6d (12¹/₂p) per week and this arrangement only applied on the 'Brighton' section, probably a legacy from early 'overhead' days. However, our instructor knew his subjects and I found the training period of interest. We learned about basic electricity, to be respectful of the unseen and deadly force, the equipment protected by fuses of varying amperage rating, control circuits, how to 'cut in' and 'cut out' the knife switches when the units were in the depots, and most important of all, the Westinghouse brake, of which I knew very little.

Those old units which I eventually drove were known as 'nutcrackers'. There was no heating in the cabs, the only warmth coming from the resistances at the back of one's head. During the winter the cabs did not become warm until the unit had been in traffic for an hour or two, whilst in the hot weather the cabs became unbearably hot. This necessitated opening the window on the right side front which created a most unhealthy draft and stirred up volumes of dust around the equipment. For safety reasons, the carriage cleaning staff were not supposed to enter the driving cabs, so by and large they were generally filthy. The motor-man's seat was a circular disc attached to the entry door and wasn't exactly the epitome of comfort. But at least I did get away from the per-petual shunting jobs on occasion, and I had the satisfaction of running passenger trains, even on the 'Pompey' main line with the 12-car "Nelsons" when the braking of those trains was considered something of an art! I well remember one day at Woking when I was learning the road to Portsmouth, a senior driver from either Alton or Portsmouth (Fratton depot) had made the detachment of the 'Pompey' portion of the Alton train when I joined him in his cab – a total stranger to me "Learning the road mate?" he asked. I replied in the affirmative. "Been down before?" "Yes", I replied, "a couple of times". "Good" said he, "I'm going into the first compartment, bash on the panel if you want me". I was somewhat surprised, to say the least at being accorded this treatment! The usual thing to happen after exchanging the normal pleasantries was that one would be invited to drive the train whilst the driver would offer advice and point out various things relating to gradients, curves and the general running of trains over the line. One thing about being 'plunged in at the deep end' so unexpectedly was that if I made a mistake it would forever be imprinted upon my memory, and it speaks volumes for the confidence that driver had, especially in a youthful man like myself. I'm pleased to say we arrived in Portsmouth L.L. without incident, and my mentor merely observed, "It's the best way to learn, do the job on your own."

The third, or live rail had been part and parcel of my footplate life in the London area so I was familiar with it and the dangers it held. This was emphasised when the correct method of using the short circuiting bar was demonstrated and practised. After the initial training period came the six weeks of road learning (which now seems incredibly short by modern standards!) and then came my first Sunday on duty on the electrics, beginning with a trip to Effingham Junction and return. On the second leg I put up my first 'black mark' in that I failed to make the booked stop at Clapham Junction, running through there on the 'up' fast line, giving the regulation two long blasts on the whistle to warn the shunters working on the adjacent line at the London end. I was confront-ed by one irate passenger who had intended to alight there, on arrival at Waterloo. My answer to the "please explain" note I received two days later was the well-worn theme of "timebook misread"! But by and large, I enjoyed my occasional electric work and experienced very little trouble, unlike one of my colleagues, Bill Cape. He seemed to be unlucky in that he had most things happen, like being 'gapped' (no collector shoe on the live rail) compressor failure, blown shoe beam ribbon fuses and equipment fuses etc. It is sometimes peculiar how one man gets most of the failures that are around, yet others go through years of electric train driving and do not even have to change a headcode lighting fuse!

Return to the Footplate – No. 6 Link

My brief excursion into the management side was now over and I looked forward to work on the footplate again. There had been a few changes in the roster and I now found myself in No. 6 Link, one above the Yard, and my fireman therein was named McNamara. He must have thought I was a hard taskmaster as I was continually on at him, seeking improvement in his work. Take, for instance, shunting in Clapham Yard. This was a busy area and the shunting that went on was sandwiched in between empty stock and van movements, both in and out of the Yard. Whenever shunting was in progress, particularly on the 'Puzzle' side, one had to keep a constant look-out for the flagman in case he was suspending shunting operations with a view to letting a train in or out of the yard. It was an extraordinary place – how many coaches could be stored there I do not know, but everything went in and out of the yard on two lines only. In all there were 49 tracks which all converged onto those two! A derailment in the Yard would cause delay and some hasty reforming of trains for the affected services.

On one occasion we were shunting at about 5.30am one summer Saturday, making up the last of the trains for the busy day ahead. Here I must add that all coaching shunting in Clapham Yard was done 'loose', which meant that the power brake had been released and the coaches were 'kicked off', just like freight wagons in a goods yard – Clapham Yard was one of the few places where this was done. We were making the final shunt and as I kicked off the last coach the shunter inadvertently 'pulled the road' between the two bogies so that the leading bogie went up its intended road and the trailing end went along another! Fortunately, it came to rest before becoming derailed and looking at it one was reminded strongly of a young lady standing with her legs crossed! Parts of the bogie which do not normally see daylight were exposed and there was no way we could go on to it and drag it back! "Well, that's torn it" the head shunter said "and just as we want to go home." Looking at the situation I suggested we might run round and push the coach back from the other end. This seemed feasible – if unorthodox – and the shunter pulled the necessary points to enable us to run round the coach. We pushed it back on to the one line, then ran round it once more and completed the move as was originally intended. Vigilance was the first step of keeping out of trouble in Clapham Yard and I was continually impressing young Mac with the need for it, especially when 'pulling up' towards the ground frame and its attendant flagman.

Mac had moved up into the next link and his place was taken by a very big, strong lad named Jock Kirton who was keen to learn his job. We had No. 32500, one of our Nine Elms E4 tanks, with the Westinghouse brake. They were formerly of the old LBSC Railway and in those days this one was No. 500 *Puttenham*. These 0-6-2 tanks proved ideal for this work. Towards the end of our tour of duty I became fed up with pulling the reversing lever to and fro so I said to my mate, "Come over here Jock, you can have a little go". Only too pleased he came across to have a turn at driving. He 'pulled up' with a three-coach set and the shunter prepared to knock this off, giving Jock the required hand signals. The E4 was reversed, Jock opened the regulator and kicked off the coaches. On receiving the stop signal, Jock closed the regulator, or so he thought; in fact it did not close. I jumped up off his seat after assessing the situation, opened the regulator wide, then immediately closed it. But meantime, we had followed that three-coach set and collided smartly with it. The coal in our bunker leapt out at the crash and sprayed onto the shunter's 'runner' (a riding truck), the oil feeder and 'thick pot' in the 'dish' jumped out and deluged us with oil! After the crash, and when the dust had settled, I asked Jock if he was all right? Fortunately no one was hurt but the coaching stock sustained damage and this meant the incident needed to be reported.

In submitting my report I stated that the main valve of the regulator had been opened inadvertently during shunting and had remained open until the regulator was opened wide, and then successfully closed, thus regaining control of the locomotive. Several days later the Chief Locomotive Inspector beckoned me over, "Laddie" said he, "I've had the regulator on 32500 examined and there is nothing wrong with it!" Defending myself I replied, "I didn't report a defect in the regulator, merely that it had been opened inadvertently on to the big valve and, as you know, once that has happened it must be opened wide before it can be closed." He grunted, said very little more and stalked away, and that was the end of that little incident. Thereafter, Jock moderated his strength in order to be able to feel a slight 'stop' prior to opening up the main valve of an E4 regulator.

Prior to the introduction of these 'Brighton' engines to Clapham Yard the shunting engines were normally the Adams 0-4-4 tanks with a steam brake. Really, they were totally unsuited for the heavy stopping work required when shunting with long rakes of coaches. On occasion an M7 class 0-4-4T might be on the duty, and these were fitted with the vacuum brake, and as the shunter's runner was also vacuum fitted, this would be piped up to add a little more to the poor braking power of the M7s. Some drivers would reverse the engine when not stopping quickly enough but this tended to make the piston glands blow, being a practice recommended for use only in emergency. On rare occasions a G6 class 0-6-0 tank would appear and shunting thereafter became an easier occupation as the brake was much better, with the whole weight of the loco available for adhesion. I liked Jock Kirton for he was interested in the work but he was called up for National Service, after which he returned to the railway for a short time only as he obtained a job in Kingston Power Station close to his home. The last time I saw him was when he was on his way for National Service. I happened to get 'caught' for a main line turn and Jock just happened to be on the train!

Main Line Opportunities

I always kept my eye open for any opportunity to go on the main line and when such a chance presented itself I seized it with both hands. I must add this was somewhat to the disdain of some of the older main line drivers who felt that young drivers should not have been permitted on such work. Another driver, Bert Fordrey was in the same position as myself and he too would opt for a gallop down the main line when able to do so.

During 1953 a 'Merchant Navy', No. 35020 *Bibby Line*, broke her crank axle near Crewkerne and consequently the whole 30 engines of the class were temporarily withdrawn pending sonic tests on the axles. This presented difficulties for the motive power departments on all sections where the 'Merchant Navys' were running and some loco's were hurriedly borrowed from other regions. Several Thompson B1s went to Stewarts Lane Depot, whilst Nine Elms acquired some Gresley V2 2-6-2s from King's Cross. I would have loved to have had a trip on one of those, in fact, I did not even have to do any of the shed preparation or disposal work during their period on the Southern Region. However, during this interesting period I was 'spare' at Nine Elms and received instructions to go 'pass' to Willesden Loco and bring back a Stanier "Black 5" for service.

My mate and I went to Willesden High Level via Richmond and walked to the sheds. I approached the R/F there and he informed us that engine No. 45061 had not yet arrived, "she should be going by in a few moments into Euston on a train from Manchester", he told us. Sure enough the "Black 5" went galloping by a minute or two later, but it was an hour or more before it got to the Loco Yard. When it did, we climbed aboard and made ourselves known to the pilotman. A quick check was made of the water level in the tender, we then went out of the depot to Mitre Bridge Junction. Here, the pilotman asked if I would be all right. "Yes" I answered, somewhat puzzled. "I can walk back quite easily from here, but it's awkward to get back from Kensington." The reason for his question was now obvious and I hastened to assure him I would be all right on my own to Kensington. So that was it, and with him gone we went on our way and I enjoyed this short spell on a strange engine – a class I had heard so much about. The injectors were no trouble and we got to Nine Elms without any fuss. I saw our foreman, told him what I had brought for service, and he said, "Is she alright? For goodness sake don't 'stop' her Bert, I want her for the 3.54pm this afternoon." I answered, "45061 hasn't said anything derogatory to me on the way home from Willesden and the firebox shows no sign of leaking anywhere." We disposed of the 4-6-0 and I told my mate not to open the smokebox door as it was self cleaning. No point in looking in there unless the engine wasn't steaming, in which case the shields of the self cleaning apparatus might have become dislodged. The ash that would be in there would be negligible, only up against the door itself but would be cleaned out if the engine was booked to be 'washed out'. So that was left and with the fire banked up, the ashpan raked out, we left her. I never saw this "Black 5" after that, but she went into traffic along with the V2s.

Those 'foreign' engines were liked by some of our chaps and were 'take it or leave it' by others. To those drivers who liked a longish cut-off and small regulator opening the V2s were not very popular, for they were basically engines which lent themselves to full regulator and short cut-off working. This method of driving would certainly get them over the ground and for the chaps who drove their engines like that they were quite popular. Firemen had difficulty on some occasions, maintaining the boiler as it was not long before the hard coals on the tender had all gone, replaced with the second grade Welsh coal supplied to Nine Elms. This required engines to be 'drafted' to burn it or, exceptionally careful and expert firing was needed to get the best results. The Exeter coal hopper was notorious for pounding up the Welsh coal into dust, and as the V2 tenders did not have a built in water spray, the task of keeping down the dust proved something of a problem. The crews would arrive at their destination looking more like chimney sweeps than enginemen as the coal watering hose only worked off the live steam injector on the driver's side of the foot plate. This was the one not normally used, and this was probably done deliberately to make sure that the injector was used occasionally. A short coal watering hose and high open tender front did not lend itself to efficient laying of the Welsh dust. But by and large the V2s acquitted themselves on our express work very well, although one man in particular, Gerry Sartin, for whom I had the highest regard as a competent engineman, said to me, "Bert, they're crude engines, after a 'West Country'!" Following their return to the ER I sometimes wondered what the King's Cross enginemen thought of the 'blind coal' on the tenders, after their Yorkshire 'hards'!

Gerry also worked on the "Black 5s", having one on the 3.30pm to Bournemouth and return three times in one week, and maintained it was the most economical locomotive he had ever worked on. Praise indeed from a true LSWR man used to the Drummond inside cylinder 4-4-0s and latterly the 'Schools' when they went to Bournemouth Depot after the Portsmouth electrification in 1937. Gerry fired regularly on No. 926

Repton when on the Bournemouth Top Link and came to Nine Elms during the war to take up appointment as driver.

MIC

I joined the Mutual Improvement Class (MIC) early in my career at New Cross Gate where our instructor was driver Harry Bucknole (always known as Sam). Colloquially known as 'knocks and blows' he began his career on the railway as a cleaner at Nine Elms in 1908 and went to 'The Gate' for driving appointment in 1928, so he was a 'Drum's man.' But Sam knew the engine and rules exceptionally well and was full of anecdotes illustrating various rules applied under certain circumstances. On learning of my transfer to fireman at Nine Elms in 1940 Sam wished me well and said I would do well there. But because of the exigencies of war the MIC movement at my new depot was non-existent. However, as soon as hostilities ceased the MIC began to function once again and I was grateful for that, using the room set aside in Brunswick House at Vauxhall for our meetings.

Two very keen men from Stewarts Lane had arrived at Nine Elms in 1944 for promotion to drivers, namely Fred Prickett and Fred Coombes. Their knowledge of locomotives and rules appeared to be limitless and there is no doubt in my mind that I, along with other chaps of similar seniority, reaped great benefit from their guidance. This enabled us to pass the driving examination in February 1947 at the first attempt. It was a point of honour to pass first time, but if a failure, a second attempt would be made after three months. If still no success another try would come along six months later – and if still a failure then one would be removed from the line of footplate promotion and given a labouring job in the shed.

Some men had to do a fair bit of 'cramming' when their time to take the examination approached, especially if they had had a failure. Fred Coombes went on to the 'electrics' after a few years but Fred Pickett remained at Nine Elms until it closed and finally retired from Waterloo. He then began to take an active interest in the Merchant Navy Locomotive Preservation Society (MNLPS) who own No. 35028 *Clan Line*, giving unstintingly of his time and knowledge until he died in 1982. Fred ran an MIC at his home in Worcester Park for the benefit of the society members and undoubtedly helped to make the MNLPS one of the best run of its kind in the country. He was a popular and often witty man with the society members, giving a dignity, (sometimes lacking in our fraternity), to his approach to their many problems, and solutions. Another valued and respected society member is Jack Finch, former boilermaker chargehand at Nine Elms, and it goes without saying that Fred Prickett's guidance can be seen today as the society members go about their allotted tasks when *Clan Line* is running special trains on BR.

I too, kept going to the MIC at Nine Elms, and when the classroom at Brunswick House was closed we were allocated a room in the 'Clock

Tower', formerly the drawing office of Joseph Beattie. The room had been renovated, the equipment transferred from the former classroom and the management encouraged us by supplying drawings, notebooks, a sectionalised injector and other items when requested. I was the Class Chairman for many years and George Burton and Tim Crowley were the secretaries at various times, both going on beyond driving to become footplate inspectors.

BR ran a nationwide MIC quiz in the 1950s and during that decade the movement reached its highest post-war level. Sadly though, with the decline of steam, interest in the MIC waned and the scheme was closed down due to lack of interest and support in the early 1960s. In 1959 BR ran a three week course at Faverdale Hall, Darlington to teach MIC instructors how to 'get their message across' – not the subjects but how to make things interesting for those who wanted to learn. There were 20 enginemen there from depots up and down the country, as far afield as Plymouth, South Wales, Wigan, Manchester, Doncaster and Southend. Another driver from Nine Elms – Frank Holloway and I, were requested to attend and it turned out to be a somewhat unique gathering. This was the only time an entire course was given over to 20 drivers and firemen who ran their own MICs. We were Course 58 and every one got on remarkably well with one another and with the Faverdale instructors. Since then we have had reunions in London every November with usually ten to twelve attending, even now we have the gentle 'dig' at one another over the respective locomotives of the four old main line companies and seldom discuss diesels or electrics. The new 'set up' merits discussion, but not always complimentary to BR whilst the disappearance of the old Motive Power Dept., is very much deplored on all sides.

We used to travel to Darlington on the Monday of each week and return home on Saturday morning. On one occasion I applied for, and obtained a footplate pass to ride up from Darlington to King's Cross. For the first stage of the journey we had an A3 Pacific and the driver was a taciturn man from 'Top Shed'. Approaching Newark he whistled up and said he intended to have another engine from Grantham. "What's wrong with this one?" I asked. "She is not using enough oil in the front end" was his reply. So, on arrival there we changed over to a V2, watched by the Grantham R/F, to whom the driver reported the defect on the A3. On changing footplates I asked if I might do the firing and both men were quite happy to let me have a go. There was plenty of water in the glass and I pulled the fire through with the pricker as we left, letting it burn until it was incandescent. The boiler primed a little for a start but then she cleared herself and began to superheat, going up the bank to Stoke Summit. The coal was small but hard, just like kitchen cobbles and I wedged my back against the handbrake standard and began a systematic firing all round the firebox. I hardly put down the shovel, just feeding the fire almost casually, the boiler pressure stood on 220 psi (working pressure) and the exhaust injector was a joy, maintaining half a glass of water. The V2 was skimming along on a short cut-off and well open regulator, and I began to enjoy the experience, for it was in good condition and galloped along in good style. The driver became almost affable and as we approached Huntingdon, he suggested I had better let his mate run her in to King's Cross as I might have too much fire on. "I've only got about six inches all over the grate" I said, but his reply was "You may have more than that, as you've not put the shovel down". "Yes" I agreed, "but I was only feeding it in at the rate she was burning it." Nevertheless, the fireman took over and he completed the run into the 'Cross' and that was my sum experience of the class.

On the Saturday of the same week that I had brought No. 45061 to Nine Elms from Willesden, I was 'spare' in the shed, and a driver failed to appear for a Southampton job and the foreman asked if I was all right for Southampton. "Not half" I answered. "Right, 34063, get her ready and away you go, your mate is Ron Feltham." This was *229 Squadron* and our train was one of the few Bournemouth ones which were booked via Ringwood. We were relieved by an Eastleigh crew at Southampton, having accomplished the art of 'stopping right' for water in a satisfactory manner and came home 'on the cushions'. I thought to myself that it had not been too bad a week.

An Experiment in Water Economy

Several weeks later, I was on a turn which involved working a 70-wagon (loaded) freight from Feltham Yard to Nine Elms Goods, and on this particular morning, I had a main line fireman named Jack Saunders, Charlie Letchford's regular mate. Before we left I asked him, "Do you think it's possible to work this train right through to Nine Elms on one fire and one boilerful of water?" He said he did not think so, but I suggested we try it. So, as we stood on the train in Feltham Yard, John filled the boiler up above the top nut of the gauge glass on our loco – No. 30524, one of the Maunsell H15s. Next, he put a good amount of coal into the firebox, level with the lip of the door and sloping evenly towards the front of the grate. At that I said, "We'll make that do John, see how we go." We were allowed 22 minutes to pass Brentford, an almost ridiculously lengthy timing, and on receiving the 'tip' to start, I took the train out of the yard very gently, leaving the cylinder drain cocks open. I did not close them until we passed Hounslow Junction and we just toodled along barely using any steam. Even so, I could not spin out the time past Brentford any longer than 20 minutes. Round the corner at Kew, under clear signals but approaching Chiswick box, a green flag held steadily by the signalman indicated that the usual 'Block regulation 5' was in operation to Barnes Junction, which meant that the section was clear but the station or junction was blocked. So we needed to regulate the speed of the train to accommodate a possible stop at the outer home for Barnes. We made slow progress up the rise to Barnes Bridge to avoid having to stop at that signal which would have meant 'buffering up' the train on a falling gradient to the dip in the road, prior to entering the platform, a not altogether desirable situation. So 'hang back' and allow time for the 'up' suburban and Reading trains to clear Barnes, after which we would 'get the road'. The outer home, 'off', came into view sighting the 'inner home' almost immediately, also 'off', and now I knew the platform starter and advance would also be clear and I could now give 30524 a 'bit of stick'. The couplings had to be kept out taut on the 70 wagons to avoid a snatch when the engine began to climb out of the dip with its tendency to slow down, counteracted by giving her another nick or two on the lever.

When I estimated the whole of the train was on the now rising gradient towards Putney, I was able to ease the loco on slightly undulating ground now until the dip which had to be negotiated in similar fashion through Clapham Junction. This was also managed without the slightest sign of a 'snatch'. I closed the regulator at West London Junction to coast into Nine Elms Goods, the water in the gauge glass dropped to one inch (it would 'lift' around an inch or two when the regulator was opened) and John asked, "Have you finished your experiment Bert? I want to get some more water into the boiler!" I acknowledged no coal at all had been added to the fire on the journey, John keeping her quiet with intelligent use of the dampers and halfdoor. So we did prove it was possible to work 70 loaded 'Vanfits' from Feltham Yard to Nine Elms Goods without adding coal or water. Other drivers I knew, said this was impossible, but with planning and careful use of the locomotive in the early stages of the journey to avoid priming it was surprising what could be done!

Southampton Docks

On Saturday 29th July 1953 I was again booked 'spare', and this time the R/F asked, "Are you all right for the New Docks?" I nodded, and he went on, "Bosco Mills hasn't shown up yet, start to get 34059 ready and if he does not get here, away you go." So I hurried to find *Sir Archibald Sinclair* where Al Butcher was well advanced with his side of the preparation, and oiled around, hoping that Bosco would not arrive before we left! Out of the shed and down to No. 1 pit to top up with water and coal, still the main line driver was missing and the foreman came over, "Right away Bert, take her light to Eastleigh, from the Docks" he called out. I acknowledged and 'blew up' for the shed exit signal, well pleased at the thought of another trip down the main line. Despite having a 13-coach load the timing of 58 minutes to pass Worting junction (51 miles from Waterloo) was leisurely.

The bucket tap on the tender front was the engineman's usual guide to the water situation. It was usual to 'try to tap' anywhere from Winchfield onwards and if one could draw water at Basingstoke then that was considered economical enginemanship. On this occasion we had 'water in the tap' just before we went into the first tunnel at Lichfield (now

Roundwood) an indication of an excellent trip. One of my former drivers, Sam Mills, who was on the 9.30am to Bournemouth that morning, was on the 'down' local line at Southampton taking water when we went slowly past on the main line. Sam's mate, Harry Vincent, called out to him, "Look who's there!" Sam saw me and waved, Harry evidently thinking it hilarious that a young driver should be working a boat train. After leaving the train in the New Docks we went 'light' to Eastleigh Loco, where I reported to the R/F, he asked me, "Where's your driver?" I answered, "I am the driver!" – he looked startled, "Oh well, leave her there and catch your train home." I hasten to add that although I was 37 at the time, I was a young driver and looked somewhat youthful! We have to remember that only a few years previously we had main line firemen who were 40 years of age plus, and within my own link (No. 6) there were these same chaps, now drivers, who were 14 years senior to me, and that much older also.

A point of interest about going into and out of the Docks was that the signal controlling entry therein was operated by a Docks pilotman-cum-shunter, who pulled the necessary points and flagged you over the numerous road crossings within the docks. Sometimes it was ten minutes from the time you entered the dock gates to the time you actually came to a stand in the allotted berth. Southampton Docks at that time was an extremely interesting place and a hive of activity. Transatlantic travel was still very much with ocean liners and air travel as we know it today was still unknown.

On Guard's Duties

On one occasion, in March 1954, there was an electric train 'off the road' in Durnsford Road electric depot (Wimbledon) and the breakdown crew was sent out to man the breakdown train, the time being about 2.30am. But, unfortunately, a guard was not available anywhere so the R/F asked me to act as the guard. I agreed to this but said, "I'll need some guard's Wrong Line Orders (WLO), both the white and pink forms". The foreman looked at me with some consternation but he knew I was right in requesting them. Detonators, and red and green flags with a hand-lamp would be readily available within our own stores. He telephoned to Nine Elms Goods Yard and asked if they could produce a set of guard's WLOs but they could not. All the guards had their own supply and there was none available at that hour of the night. Slight consternation! However, it seemed delay to the breakdown train was becoming rather lengthy and as the probabilities of having to use a WLO were remote, I elected to go along without the forms, but it was an interesting situation and the incident was logged. Thereafter, the pink and white WLO forms were on hand in the depot. This was the only time I ever acted as a guard and the experience proved interesting. I had to make sure the train was marshalled correctly, with the crane travelling next to the engine, testing the brakes, etc.

Awkward Duty Times

I was always keen to get out on the running road and to do this I would change over for awkward times of duty. As I lived only twelve minutes' walk from the depot, very early turns did not concern me very much, provided I was going out on the 'iron road'. So, on occasion I found myself on the Ascot Parcels which involved booking on at 2.57am, preparing an engine, usually a D15 class 4-4-0, and running light to Waterloo to work the 4.20am to Ascot and Woking via Camberley. After stabling the train at Woking we would go light to Guildford Loco and leave the engine there prior to travelling home passenger. I would give away a more amenable time on duty in order to do this work. One such turn was the 8am, going 'pass' to Clapham Yard for carriage shunting on an E4. During this period the engine would be taken to Nine Elms Loco for servicing, ie. fire and ashpan cleaned, coal bunker topped up, sand boxes filled and engine oiled, plus any minor fitter's work such as piston glands blowing, brake adjusting etc., before returning to the fray of Clapham Yard.

A Dead Stop at Fleet

On Whit Saturday 1954 I was booked for a Salisbury turn with Harry English, a fireman in the Top Link. We signed on at 10.25am for 10.40 off the shed, the engine having been prepared by another set of men. No. 34061 (which came brand new to Nine Elms from Brighton Works in 1947) was worked up to Waterloo for the 11.15am special to the West of England, the last of the many divisions of the 'A.C.E.'. I asked Harry, "Which way would you like to do the driving?", and he replied, "On the 'down'." So having coupled on, Harry created the brake, I adjusted the headcode, we had a cup of the brew and left right time at 11.15am. Harry made an excellent job of the driving, as I knew he would. He did his share with Joe McCarthy, his driver on the Top Link, whilst I had an enjoyable trip as the fireman. On arrival at Salisbury, Harry 'spotted' the locomotive under the water column, and we then automatically reverted to our proper roles of driver and fireman. The Exeter driver, named Billings, was waiting to relieve us, and he watched Harry make the stop then immediately scramble up on the back of the tender to hold in the pipe whilst he turned on the water. I picked up the oil feeder and went around the sides of *73 Squadron* to feel the bearings and top up the slide bars and gland cups. I came back on the platform, gave Driver Billings the load and tonnage, he looked at me and then Harry, and to the day he retired I do not think he knew which of us was really the driver!

We had some two or three hours at Salisbury before our return, so we had a walk around a park and the delightful town. On returning to the station I chatted with a Salisbury driver as our train rolled in with No. 34057 on the front. "She gets over the ground all right", he observed, "but there's plenty of clatter around the sides," meaning play in the coupling rod and big end bushes. The tender was topped up and some coal pushed forward and we set off, booked to call at Andover and Woking. Under the watchful eye of the Salisbury driver I managed to make a clean start, always difficult at Salisbury with eleven coaches. We galloped up the bank, through Porton and over the top at Grateley, then swooped down the gradient into Andover. I thought the Salisbury driver had described *Biggin Hill* well, but we got going again and went by Worting Junction on time. We sailed on through Basingstoke under clear signals and I was enjoying all that I surveyed. Approaching Fleet at around 80 mph there was a sudden very heavy 'knock' from the front end, accompanied by a cloud of steam. I did not know quite what to do for a second or two – there were bits falling off the engine and I could hear them striking various parts as we went along.

I eased the regulator and Harry called out, "Don't shut off Bert". I did not, but gave the brake handle a steady downwards push destroying about ten inches of brake, which brought us to a stand about a quarter mile from Fleet home signal, closing the regulator as we stopped. I got down and checked around the engine. Outside everything was normal, so I stood by the front buffer and called out to Harry "Give her a bit of steam". He did so and I was nearly blown away by the force of it! Returning to the footplate, I spoke to my fireman, "I reckon we've got a hot middle big-end Harry, which has given enough play to knock out the front cylinder cover. We shall have to have assistance." "Right," he said, "I'll go back and tell the guard you are going to issue a wrong line order." "That's the drill mate", I said, so Harry nipped back to tell the guard we were a failure and to take his 'dets' and protect the train. In the meantime I prepared the green WLO addressed to the signalman at Fleet, stating that we were a failure and needed assistance, and to please send a locomotive back 'wrong line' to where we were standing. Harry returned and reported that the guard had gone back to protect. "I'll not walk up the track Bert, I'll go up the road to the station". This ran parallel with the railway on the downside, so he vaulted the fence, went through an alleyway between some cottages and disappeared.

It was a hot sultry day, and after adding some more water to the boiler to keep her quiet as long as possible, I got down again. A passenger spoke to me from the leading coach, "What's up driver?" he asked. I answered, "The old girl's falling to pieces." "I thought so," said he, "There was something striking the underneath of this coach." I looked under and there were one or two marks clearly visible where something heavy had struck. I returned to the footplate as all the London bound traffic was beginning to come up the local line, adjacent to the main line. After about half-an-hour, the guard returned, and I asked him, "What are you doing here?" "Well driver," he said, "I got back to the automatic signal in the rear and there was a train already standing on it. I telephoned the signalman who asked me to remind the crew of that train to protect it, and then rejoin my own train, and here I am." "Oh, all right," I answered, as under normal circumstances, the guard would have had to remain at the automatic signal until a train arrived and stopped at it (but it had already), or was recalled from protection duties by the driver. We chatted for a few moments then one of the occupants of the cottages called out, "Would you like a jug of tea?" "Yes please" I replied, so after a few moments it appeared, the guard going across to collect it – a jug of tea on a tray with two cups and some sugar, this went down most acceptably.

After a further period of time a light engine came up, a T9, the driver stopping by us, "We're your change over engine" he called out. I acknowledged, "My mate is up in Fleet box, he's got the Wrong Line Order." "Right-o," he said, and went up to the station. A few moments later the T9 dropped back on to us and the fireman coupled up. Harry, my mate, had ridden back on the engine so he quickly rejoined me. The 4-4-0 dragged us up into the station, where there were no platforms on the through line, but we stopped inside the starting signal, the brake was destroyed and Harry uncoupled *Biggin Hill* from the train. The T9 pulled up and reversed us into a siding behind the signal box where we gathered up our belongings and changed footplates. I appraised the Basingstoke driver of our misadventure as he took charge of the Bulleid Pacific. Harry and I boarded the T9 which then came out of the siding on to the 'up' fast line and back on to our train. The guard had rejoined the train when the assisting engine arrived, and Harry recoupled us to the train. I created the brake and at last we were on our way once again, some 80 minutes late. My mate gave the fire on our new charge a good 'rux-up' and she performed reasonably well. She had been station pilot at Basingstoke and the footplate was commendably clean, the copper and brass polished. We made our booked call at Woking and then there was the last sprint into Waterloo. One passenger, a little lady getting on in years, came up and thanked us for a safe arrival and expressed surprise that such a little engine could pull such a long train!

It later transpired that No. 34057 had not suffered what I had thought. The middle big-end was perfectly all right, but the castle nut on the piston head had slackened back on the thread which had resulted in the very heavy knock that we had heard. The loose piston head had subsequently sheared the threads so that the nut flew off, the piston head followed suit and knocked off the front cylinder cover which itself became lodged in the aperture, and that in itself was fortunate. The cover was broken of course, and it was pieces of this that I had heard bouncing along under the engine. The steam chest casting had fractured in three places so when she eventually arrived in Eastleigh Works for repairs, a substantial amount of work needed to be undertaken. So, I was only partly correct with my assumption of what had gone wrong. Afterwards, when thinking about the job, and one is always wise in hindsight, I should have let the engine coast until we were in station limits at Fleet, and thus avoided the use of a Wrong Line Order but this was the only one I ever issued!

One main line driver – Bill Woods, was kind enough to ask me what had happened, so I told him about it, he said, "I thought Bert, that you had knocked someone down on that footcrossing half-a-mile back". "No Bill, it was a mechanical failure", to which he opined, "I expect some of the chaps will say you shouldn't have been there and that it wouldn't have happened to them!" My reply was, "Well, that of course Bill, is all eyewash, it would have happened even if the Royal Train driver had been in charge." He agreed.

One small item which had expedited the proceedings was that when Harry got on the road to walk up to the station, a police car had stopped and the driver asked, "Where are you going?" Harry replied, "Up to the station to get some assistance, our engine has just come to grief." "Jump in" said the policeman, "I'll run you up to the station." So my mate had a lift which must have saved at least ten minutes and, as a member of the MIC he knew just what to do in the circumstances. Most Top Link firemen would have the necessary knowledge of the rules to do the same without any prompting from the driver, because of being senior men they would be preparing themselves to pass the driving examination.

An Excursion from Willesden

On Saturday 24th July I was booked on a most interesting job. This was 12.20am with the engine prepared by Tom Banton and his mate for the 12.35am off the shed light engine to Willesden to take on a holiday train, and work it to Portsmouth Harbour. Now my electric work was 'bearing fruit'. The engine provided was three-cylinder U1 class No. 31908. At Clapham Junction our Stewarts Lane pilotman came aboard and we went tender first up to Willesden, at that time a veritable maze of sidings and signals, in true LNWR tradition. We settled in a small bay platform awaiting the arrival of our train which was coming from the North Midlands. The platform foreman came along and said, "Your train will be here in about 40 minutes" so our pilot driver volunteered to go and make a can of tea. Our tender was loaded up with some good Welsh coal so I said to my mate, Bob King, "Let's have a nob up". He was willing so I removed the baffle plate from the firehole with the shovel and Bob handed me the lumps and I placed them by hand in the back corners and down the sides, building up a high wall of coal at the 'back end' of the firebox. When I deemed we had enough in there I replaced the baffle plate, and when I did so the lumps were nestling against the sides of it. After this was done the footplate was washed down and made 'spic and span'. I commented to Bob, "You'll only need to fire down the sides for miles". "Fine," he replied.

Our driver returned with the tea, and as we enjoyed a cup, the fire was burning up slowly as only soft coal can. Soon our train arrived and one of the ubiquitous "Black 5s" came off and we went back on; Bob coupled on and a brake was created, tested, then right away to Clapham Junction where our pilotman left us. Onward again, over the East Putney line to join the main line at Wimbledon, and by this time that

Welsh coal was really alight. The boiler pressure stood on the 200 psi 'red line' and Bob thought it was marvellous. The Maunsell engine was going well. I liked the U1s as they rode much more steadily than the U class two-cylinder variety of 2-6-0s which had a tendency 'to hunt' when running hard, the reason for imposing a 70 mph limit. We called at Guildford to top up the tender tank and set off again, but going up the 1 in 80 of Haslemere Bank, Bob 'lost' his fire. He had not fed it quite sufficiently and she began to lose pressure and by the time we turned the bank summit the boiler pressure was down to 150 psi. The water was fairly low in the glass but I was able to ease the engine right back on the down grades to Petersfield and instructed Bob to build up the fire again under the door and back corners, which he did, and thereafter we had no further falling off of boiler pressure.

All in all it was a good trip and I enjoyed it, as like myself as a young driver, Bob was a young fireman and needed the experience. There was one thing I had to consider on this morning and that was, that whilst I had a fair knowledge of the Portsmouth road when it came to driving electric trains, the working of a steam engine over the line was an entirely different proposition, especially with an inexperienced fireman. I had done but very little firing over the road, so therefore I did not have the same familiarity as I had with the Salisbury and Bournemouth lines. Therefore, working a steam engine in the dark I did not desire to take charge of the firing side of the job until it was absolutely essential. To do this would mean looking into the firebox to see the condition of the fire and when one looks in there for several seconds, then upon looking out of the side of the locomotive immediately afterwards, one cannot see a thing for a moment or so. Thus it would be essential that a look in the firebox would have to be reduced to just a glance. Faced with a similar situation on the road to either Salisbury or Bournemouth, I could tell just where I was with much more ease than on the Pompey line, so I repeat, I was still learning as was my mate!

Frustration in No. 6 Link

During my years in No. 6 Link I found it frustrating at times. I wanted main line work, but as was usual in large depots, that was the province of the senior links. Within my own link were drivers some 15 years senior to me and ever since they had been on the railway, they had been left behind in the quality of work they were called upon to perform. When they did eventually get to main line firing some did not then want it, and were content to potter along on any little job. When they became drivers, any ambition they may have had, had been whittled away and so they were content to accept the humdrum jobs without any looking forward to main line work. Of course, not all the men were the same, some chaps just accepted whatever came their way and made the best of it, whilst I was always on the lookout for 'a runner' and seized the opportunity when it presented itself.

Here, I must say that I considered the men who started on the footplate around 1920 had the 'dirty end of the stick' all their lives. Years of cleaning, then firing, often becoming too old to do main line firing continuously, spending years on 'housetop' driving jobs and by the time main line driving came their way they had lost interest. The 1923 Grouping, the coming of the motor bus and car, all took their toll as there was an insidious loss of work only stemmed by the Second Great War, after which the gradual diminishing amount of transport work affected us all. I went back on the Nine Elms goods link for a period due to roster adjustments by the 'razor gang', (a group of men whose task in life was to look around to see what little job could be cut out!). In fact, I was the junior rostered driver on the sheets, and while appointed drivers behind me were not back firing, they needed to see their following day's work shown on the daily alteration sheet. I think the biggest single factor in our work loss, apart from the 1955 Modernisation Plan, was when the railways ceased to be 'common carriers', resulting in the closure of marshalling yards and station yards alike. Due to economic pressures the only freight work BR was now interested in was bulk loads, and gone for ever was the small local goods train, dropping off wagons of coal and the 'road box' wagons in the unloading sheds, picking up the empties to be taken to the marshalling yards and then returned to their source of supply. Coal fired generating stations were phased out in favour of oil and nuclear energy, all making for another nail in the railwayman's coffin.

Before the summer service of 1954 had finished, I did get another job to Salisbury on Saturday 14th August. I was booked 7am 'spare' and the foreman asked, "Was I all right for Salisbury?" I answered, "Of course". "Away you go," he instructed, "Vic Rowe is your fireman" and on this occasion we had a Urie Arthur, No. 30745 *Tintagel*. We called at Woking then right away to Salisbury, but on passing milepost 31 at the summit of the drag from Woking, I pulled her up too short on the cutoff, lessening the blast on the fire too much so that she went 'off the boil'. Thereafter with that class of engine I invariably put the regulator back on to the 'first valve' leaving the cut-off around 30 per cent on running ground and this kept the firemen happy. Another little lesson learned and stored away. On 18th September I was booked to work the 6pm Exeter as far as Salisbury as the roster clerk was unable to cover the turn with a main line driver. So I fell in for the job, much to my surprise and delight. The engine booked for this duty was an Exeter 'Merchant Navy', my fireman was Tommy Ball, and after preparing the engine we went light to Waterloo to hook on to the usual twelve coaches. The MN was one of the first ten with a Drummond steam reverser and was in good condition, as Exeter engines usually were. We had an excellent trip with Tom pressing me 'to have a go' – "I don't mind shovelling coal Bert," he called out, so I 'opened the old girl up a bit' and she was soon running before time, which often courts signal delays. There is no point in doing that, it's different if one has had a late start, the incentive is there to win back time, and a 'Merchant Navy' could certainly do that. After relief at Salisbury by an Exeter crew we had our meal break and then relieved Salisbury men on the 'up' milk train destined for Clapham Junction. A Nine Elms MN was on the job, usually the one off the 11am 'A.C.E.'

The running of this train was interesting as it was quite heavy and with 20 or so tanks in tow, with the milk itself surging about, one could feel the effects it had on the drawbar. This working involved going over the East Putney line from Wimbledon to Clapham Junction, where the train was put inside, the engine uncoupled and thence it was light to Nine Elms Loco, where we were relieved by a disposal set of men. Sadly, all the milk which now comes up to London from the West Country does so on the road, but surely not as economically as by bulk rail transport.

Signing for the Road

In the matter of 'signing for the road', if one had not been over a particular road for six months, or longer, then you were quite at liberty to strike off that line from your route card. Here I must say that some drivers were meticulous in their observance of this. In my own case, I was careful that when I signed for a road which was not covered by work within my own link, I would endeavour to go over that particular line so that if anyone asked me, "When were you last at Salisbury or Bournemouth?" or wherever, I would be able to quote the dates and thus obviate any recriminations because I had worked over a road with a longer period than six months in between. It was possible to put a note in to the shedmaster requesting a refresher if one had not been over any particular road for six months. This I would do if it applied to work within my own link or within the Dual Panel, but in my position as a junior driver the roster clerk would refuse to book me a main line refresher unless it was done under the cloak of just being shown 'road refresher' without naming any particular place.

When 1955 came along this proved to be the year of discontent on the railway, culminating in a footplate strike which lasted from Sunday 29th May until Wednesday 15th June. Altogether a very unhappy period, especially as the gains were negligible. By this time a new set up in the links was beginning to take place, the old Dual Panel was discontinued and a Dual Link was introduced whereby prospective motormen progressed from the Dual Link to the electric depots. I did not choose to go this way and so my electric work finished, except for a brief interlude several months later, because the new Dual Links did not prove acceptable to the drivers and there was a shortage of electric trained men. The management fondly hoped the old Dual Panel men would elect to form the nucleus of the new link, but it did not happen! So we were requested to take up the spare electric work until the Dual Link became full, mostly with young drivers as it seemed that was the only way to the driver's position. There was not a driver appointed to steam work at Nine Elms for eight or nine years. Tom Banton was our senior passed fireman for years and was always booked out driving. Then it used to take five years for a man to reach top rate driving money! An appointed man's rises would arrive via the calendar but in Tom's case he became 'top rated' before I did as his Sunday turns and 'rest days' counted – he was on his maximum several months prior to me! Such was the manner of things then.

The Diesels Arrive

Around this time, the '204' diesel mechanical shunting locomotives made their appearance. Weighing about a hopeless 27 tons, and powered by 204 horsepower engines which became much sought after in later years by owners of pleasure craft. These locomotives proved totally inadequate for heavy shunting duties – a brake van was heavier! A long draft of wagons needed real power for starting and stopping, and it was a relatively busy job as the locos had a 5-speed gearbox and when changing up the revs needed to die down before a higher gear could be engaged. All right changing down as the gear lever could be moved to engage a lower gear with full revs on. They were used on one particular section of Nine Elms Goods, namely the 'Coal Road' but they were not very popular. If the weather dictated that a deal of sand needed to be used then this would cause a drain on the air reservoir, so that on occasion, it was necessary to stop the work whilst the air pressure built up again in order to make successful gear changes.

One night the loco was to be tested on the Ewell goods and I was given the job. A footplate inspector, Ted Mulberry, was there to report on the proceedings. We set off from Wimbledon West Yard with eleven wagons of coal and a brake van. Normal progress was made along the Goods Loop to Raynes Park, then out on to the local line and immediately turned off on to the Epsom branch on a falling gradient, running in reverse gear. I managed to get her into the fifth gear with a view to having a run at the bank immediately facing us, but as soon as we were on the rising gradient the revs began to fall. I changed down to notch 4, but by the time Motspur Park was reached we were down to 3, going through Worcester Park station she was in notch 2 and shortly after, we were in bottom gear! For the remainder of the bank up to Stoneleigh we were doing 3 to 4 miles an hour. The engine was running on maximum revs and the noise created must have disturbed a few of the people sleeping in their homes close to the railway. Ted remarked, "This isn't railway work. One slip and we will have to divide the train because she will never restart on this gradient!" As we turned the top of the bank at Stoneleigh I disengaged the gear and began to coast along, immediately putting the air brake fully on after 'buffering up' the train. We sailed down the bank to Ewell West, the home signal was 'off' and I informed the inspector, "She won't stop at the home signal Ted." He agreed, so I said, "We'll try some sand," with a good carpet of the grit on the rails it was apparent the 204 would just about have stopped at the signal, but there was absolutely no margin whatsoever on the safety side, and all this was on a dry rail.

After shunting the yard at Ewell West we placed the empty wagons out on the running line, ran round the propelled out towards Epsom, over the crossover, which was reversed by the signalman, then through that to gain the 'up' line to Wimbledon West Yard. The inspector remarked, "These engines are not fit for this type of work" as he went home to bed. I did wonder who was responsible for arranging the test and who thought they would do a satisfactory job – any responsible driver would have been capable of supplying the information required without resorting to tests! Suffice to say, the 204s were not tried again on road work. There is a deal of difference pottering about with a few wagons in a naval dockyard to real work on the railway! The 350 hp diesel shunters would have made a much more successful job of that test but even so, most of the class were limited to 20 mph, which is not fast enough, even for short road goods work.

Cleanliness on the Footplate

During this long period in No. 6 Link, I had many firemen, and sometimes my rostered one was a 'passed man' and was booked out driving continuously. One such man was Jack Blanchard, and the only time I saw him, at least for working together, was on Bank Holidays when all the 'passed men' were booked firing and all the 'passed cleaners' not on the roster, were booked cleaning. So when Jack was driving, his place would be filled by cleaners or junior firemen as booked by the roster clerk. Apparently, I had a fearsome reputation amongst the younger men because I invariably insisted that things be just right on the footplate, no smoke, no blowing off, a good lookout to be maintained and last but not least, the footplate kept clean and the floorboards free of coal and dust. Dust was the one thing that I hated and I would go to any lengths to keep it down, so I always encouraged the use of the coal watering hose; dust blowing about was a hazard as it was likely to get into one's eyes and impair vision, even temporarily could be dangerous. On one occasion, whilst shunting in Clapham Yard, something entered my left eye which necessitated a visit to an eye hospital. It proved to be an 'L'-shaped piece of iron, obviously from a brake block, which had entered my eye, at about the '6 o'clock mark'. It was removed magnetically and then the wound had to be cleaned up as there was rust and other debris there – in all, I was off duty for two weeks.

One Sunday evening, whilst shunting in Clapham Yard with an E4 locomotive, the Westinghouse brake was giving trouble. One moment it would bite and the next almost useless. I concluded that there was water in the air reservoir, resolving to drain it out when the shunters went to supper. We went on the pit and I bled all the air from the system by opening the pipe cock on the bunker, and when all the air had gone, I went underneath with my small adjustable spanner and removed the drain plug on the reservoir. However, I was not smart enough to get out of the way of the cascade of water and emulsified oil which came out, propelled by about an ounce of air! My clean overalls were a horrible sight and I decided that it would be a long time before I took on a similar job with clean overalls on. Needless to say, the trouble was cleared and thereafter we had a good brake.

The BR Standards

On the first Saturday in June 1956 I had my first trip on the then new BR Standard Class 5s of which we had several at Nine Elms. I was 'collared' for a Salisbury job and the fireman was Bill Botten, later Train Crew Manager at Victoria. We went up to Waterloo and set off, first stop Salisbury. I was enjoying the trip but to my ears, accustomed to the soft beat of the Bulleid Pacifics, I thought the '5' was making a lot of noise up the chimney and I mistakenly thought I was thrashing the engine. Consequently, I treated the engine too lightly and she began to 'flag' for steam. As we approached Worting Junction with 190 psi on the clock and half a glass of water, Bill gave me a despairing look, "For cripes sake, open her up Bert!" "Okay Bill," so I pulled the regulator wide open and advanced the cutoff to 27 per cent, the engine responded and the fire began to burn more fiercely. "That's more like it. Next time you get one of these, put your ear plugs in so you can't hear her!" Well, the needle began to climb and Bill was a happier man after his good advice. Thereafter, I did not take too much notice of the 'stack music' and watched the water in the boiler and the amount of coal the fireman was burning, which is, after all, the infallible guide. I did think the BR tenders were not very special as the shovelling plate was too short and when there was plenty of coal on the tender it cascaded on to the floorboards, necessitating picking it up off the floor. When some of the coal had been used the tender became quite comfortable to work. If the shovel plate had been eight or nine inches longer, with a slightly upturned lip they would have been far better. In the main, they were relatively harsh riding engines with the steel fall-plate on the tender rubbing on the steel footplate producing plenty of noise.

No. 73110 was the best of the bunch we had at Nine Elms and I thought she was a lively, buoyant loco, eager to get on with the work. They were light on maintenance, and reliable and this carried a deal of respect from all the staff. With the graduated steam brake valve on the footplate it was possible to 'buffer up' a freight train with the minimum of effort and discomfort for the guard. Another notch on the ratchet would increase brake cylinder pressure and likewise the pressure could be graduated off, very desirable on freight work. So all in all they were true mixed traffic engines and could, within reason, take on any train we had at the Premier Depot. I did hear, through the grape vine that Percy Cox had a '5' on the 'Bournemouth Belle' on one occasion and the fireman said that he did not pull her inside 30 per cent cut-off and full regulator throughout. That fireman must have worked quite hard, as the coal consumption would have come pretty close to that of a MN to work the train, and a long narrow firebox is more difficult to fire than a wide one.

Sunday Workings

There was plenty of work about on Sundays in those days and this was dealt with by Ben Partleton. In the middle of the week he would get an idea of the work for the following Sunday ie, the additional or special work and he would cast around for footplate crews prepared to work an extra Sunday to cover the work. He came up to me one day in August and said, "I've got a nice little job for you next Sunday Bert". I rose to the bait like a fish! "Well, what is it Ben?" I asked curiously, and he answered, "On duty about 10.30am, a trooper from Kenny to Aldershot, empties back to Cannonbury – interested?" "I'll snap hold of that one Ben" I responded. "Right, your name is against that turn." quoted Ben, marching off, pleased that he had got someone to cover the job because the drivers who signed for Aldershot were 'thin on the ground', and the new breed of Dual Link men would often sign their route card 'electric work only'.

So, when the Sunday alteration sheet appeared, I was shown 10.48am with one of my former regular firemen, Freddy Elliott, currently at Wimbledon Park Depot. 11.48am off the shed, light engine to Kensington (Addison Road). We were given a U class locomotive which was prepared in the normal careful manner, footplate well cleaned and everything in 'apple pie' order. At Kensington, our train rolled in from Harwich, only seven coaches but filled with soldiers. The ex-LNER B1 came off, we went back on, the shunter coupled up, a brake was created and tested, then right away. As we were going over Chelsea Bridge, I could hear a screeching from the left hand side which appeared to come from the leading coach. I remarked to Fred that we had a hot box some-where, "Sounds like it", he replied. So we went through Clapham Junction and on to the main line at Wimbledon via East Putney. We were not very far in front of the 1.30pm to Bournemouth, but as we went by Wimbledon B box, the noise reverberated off the walls and I thought that it was getting worse. I went over to my mate's side and looked back – our middle tender axlebox was smoking! I said, "She's got to go until we go slow line at Hampton Court Junction". We pressed on but it was a relief to get on the local line as the axlebox was getting really bad. I did not regain too much speed after negotiating the crossover, but toddled on to our booked stop at Woking. The 1.30pm roared by us between Esher and Hersham, so we did not check him. When we stopped the axlebox was on fire! I drew a bucketful of hot water from the coal hose and doused the flames. I then applied a liberal dose of thick oil over the top of the box and down the horncheeks as I did not desire it to become fixed there as a seized axlebox would get you 'off the road'. I called the platform foreman, and informed him that I had a hot tender box and would take things quietly to Aldershot, when I would probably ask Control for a replacement engine.

So on we went, running quite slowly, the box making hideous noises, and on arrival at Aldershot the train was unloaded and stabled on the 'up' side. We then filled the tender tank, and with just below half a glass in the boiler, we were able to turn the engine on the rather decrepit turntable in the 'down' yard. Over to the 'up' side again and on to our train, and by this time the axlebox had cooled somewhat so I removed the cover. The sight that met my eyes was horrific; white metal with brass mixed with it was all over the place. I said to Fred, "We'll never get this one back to Nine Elms, I'll ask for another engine." So I spoke to Control and the man asked, "Can you get her to Woking?" I answered in the affirmative, "But only at 15 to 20 mph". "That's all right, follow the 3.30pm passenger train and I'll have an engine sent from Guildford to Woking – change over in the 'up' yard" he answered.

All the arrangements made were accomplished. I had further dosed up the bearing with more thick oil before leaving Aldershot, and eventually we found ourselves on another 'U boat', albeit with a dirty footplate in exchange. Because of the hasty arrangements the Guildford men had not had the time to make things presentable. However, we galloped on now, running a bit late and when we arrived at Kensington the foreman in charge asked, "What are you mate?" I replied, "Empties – Aldershot to Cannonbury, you should have a pilotman here for us." "I've seen no one, I'll 'phone Willesden Loco." was his rejoinder, but Willesden had had no intimation of the job and did not have a man there until one booked on at 6pm! My heart sank, I thought "We'll never get finished at this rate", so I said to the foreman, "I'll take the train up to the High Level and we'll pick up our pilotman there." "Thank you for that," he answered. Onwards then up to Mitre Bridge, then left up on to the High Level. Shortly afterwards our pilot driver showed up, but by this time he had some fresh orders! "These empties are to go on to Stratford". So that meant that we would have another pilotman from Cannonbury, an ER man, and eventually we arrived at Stratford around 8pm. I looked around and said to him, "I don't know how you blokes find your way around this place", to which he replied, "I don't know how you Southern blokes find your way around Clapham Junction!" So, when one is 'raised up' in vast busy areas then it all becomes second nature. However, he elected to go and make a can of tea, which was most welcome, also producing a packet of biscuits to help allay the pangs of hunger of two Southern footplatemen. Eventually we left Stratford to go light engine to Nine Elms, arriving there at 9.45 that evening. The foreman, Ted Eatwell asked, "Wherever have you been? I couldn't send relief to Clapham before you went towards Kenny because I had no one to spare." I answered, "We've been a long way from home Ted but only timewise and this will be the last time I'll work one of Ben Partleton's extras." Apart from a spoilt dinner, there was the worry that my wife suffered, as she did not know where I was as overtime of this nature had not been seen since the war. Sunday evening was just about the last time of the week when one needed to make overtime – a ruined dinner and evening. There was quite enough loss of social time associated with the ordinary hours of duty that the locomen suffered, afternoon work, very early turns and late evenings were all 'part and parcel' of the calling.

No. 3B Link – at Last

So the humdrum work of No. 6 Link went on. The Chertsey goods, Epsom and Chessington goods, Wimbledon West Yard and East Yard shunting, the Morden milk turn, Clapham Yard shunting, trips to Walton via Staines with ageing M7 tanks – each run an adventure! I wondered to myself 'whenever am I going to get promotion?' The link above mine was a tank gang which was virtually an 'old man's gang' – some of them 'green carded'. Better to remain in No. 6. The next link up from that was the Dual Link, barred to ordinary promotion, being reserved for drivers aspiring to go on electric traction, and the link beyond that was 3B, most desirable as in there they had rostered work to Salisbury and Southampton, and Bournemouth in the summer. Once in that link, the main line would be mine as a right.

I must mention George Bilyard and Vic Rowe who were rostered with me in No. 6, both passed men. George did not get booked out driving very often so when he was with me we worked 'day and day' about, sharing the driving and firing. Towards the end of 1958 there was a sudden flurry of promotion. Four moves up, the fourth one caused by Bill Cruse being appointed a Running Shift Foreman and I now found myself the junior hand in No. 3B link. At last I was a driver on the main line at Nine Elms – age 42 – to borrow a phrase from another author, "Where every prospect pleases."

2

Main Line Work

I VIEWED MY promotion to No. 3B Link with a pleasure that was closely akin to that I had when I entered number one link as fireman. There were several days enjoyed looking over the roads, particularly to Salisbury and Bournemouth and I selected the trains and their drivers with whom I had always got on well. On one occasion, I boarded the 3.30pm to Bournemouth at Basingstoke and Harry Pope, the driver, who had the reputation for hitting the engine, said to me, "Learning the roads Bert?". "That's it, Harry", I said. "Would you like to have her?" he asked. "I'd love to" I replied, to which a voice belonging to Duggie Stainer ("Squeaker"), called out, "Ruddy good job too!"

The engine was a modified 'West Country' of which we had a few, and she was relatively new from the shops. It was a sheer pleasure to handle the engine and I really enjoyed it. Harry congratulated me on our arrival in Bournemouth and I thought the fireman appreciated my efforts as well. He is currently a driver at Basingstoke and must surely be one of their older hands now.

I did go on the 8.30am to Bournemouth one morning with Dick Thomas, one of my former erstwhile vociferous complainers of young drivers working main line trains. On approaching Worting Junction I was standing behind Dick and it was necessary to view the home signal with the turnout to the Bournemouth line with the distant signal in the caution position, so it was vital to spot the home signal in good time if speed was not to be reduced, bearing in mind that the turnout was 60 mph. I followed the skyline round and spotted the necessary signal in the 'off' position. "It's off, Dick" I said. He looked at me with some astonishment, "I've never seen the signal this far back" he said. "It's off", I repeated, and immediately afterwards he saw it for himself. This sort of put him 'on his metal' because thereafter he was at pains to point out to me the best positions to catch various signals on the rest of the way to Bournemouth! On the return trip, he allowed me to drive the engine and I thought I had been accepted as almost an equal.

The fireman I had in 3B was promoted at the same time as myself. His name was Willie Rush, and he had an unenviable reputation as a fireman who could not be relied upon to do his work in a satisfactory manner, particularly when left alone to do disposal work in the depot. Chaps have told me that he had been known to open the smokebox door, and instead of emptying the contents, he merely removed one shovelful and threw it across the front platform of the engine and then closed the door. The appearance of smokebox ash on the front would give the impression that the smokebox had been emptied but that the chap doing it had failed to brush off all the ashes! Ash pans had been neglected whilst fire cleaning was done in a haphazard manner, not conducive to the free steaming of a locomotive when it was out on its next trip. With these stories in mind, I took it upon myself to watch Bill very diligently, and I would be in the vicinity when we were disposing of an engine. I checked that everything was done as I wanted it done and furthermore, expected it to be done. Out on the road Bill had the strength to wield the shovel, but did not have the necessary ideas of when and how to do it. I did not pick up the shovel on any single occasion whilst we were on the road, and he did it all under my supervision. Willie had several months with me and we managed all our running turns without a 'lost time ticket'.

In April, I was sent away for three weeks to the Darlington MIC Teacher Training Course, mentioned earlier and on my return I saw that Willie had been removed from No. 3 Link and placed in the 'Tank Gang'. He went with Bill Woods who had requested to come off main line work for a quieter job. I went in to see the Governor, Mr Gilchrist, and asked why my mate had been removed from the roster. He indicated that whilst I was on that course, my place had been filled by drivers from the main line spare link on a weekly basis, as was the usual practice. However, it appeared that two of them had complained to the Governor of the non-capabilities of Willie. I said to the Governor, "Well I haven't complained". He replied, "I know you haven't, but I have to take notice if other drivers complain". He went on, "We know this lad's reputation and we deem it advisable for him to be put in the Tank Gang". So, I had to accept the situation and when I saw Willie I said to him, "I hope you realise that I had not complained about you, your removal had nothing to do with me". He understood the position and thanked me for not complaining. I think he knew his short-comings but amazingly did nothing to improve himself. It seemed as though he expected a driver to be looking after him the whole of the time, and whenever a driver was not present he seemed to think that this was his opportunity to get away with not doing the distasteful work. There was something missing in Willie's 'make-up', and I am sure he would never have got by the inspector to become a driver, so when his family moved abroad and Willie left the railway industry, there were not many tears shed at his departure.

Vic Schofield now became my mate for a few weeks. He was an Anglo-Indian and was a prolific talker. He died in 1988 whilst in service as a driver at Slade Green, where I finished my own career and one's thoughts become sombre when a chap who was once your fireman has passed on. However, it was not long before Charlie Philpott came with me and now I really began to enjoy life. Charlie was an excellent, reliable fireman, with a zest for work and a clean footplate and we got on well together. On one occasion, we were on the 3.54pm to Basingstoke with one of the small Standards, a Class 4 2-6-0. Going by Purbright Junction we were gradually being overtaken by a boat train travelling on the through line, pulled by a Class 5 4-6-0. Charlie called out, "Don't let him pass us Bert", so I opened out this little engine a bit more and we ceased to be overtaken. We were the over takers! By the time we had gone through Canal Bridge, less than a mile further on, the Class 5 was two or three coach lengths behind and we were still gaining, but I had to shut off steam ready for the approach and stop at Farnborough. All very interesting, but we must bear in mind whereas I was hauling five coaches and a van, the Class 5 had twelve coaches and a van, a vast difference in train weight.

On Saturday, 8th August Charlie and I were rostered on duty at 9.42am to prepare a locomotive and work the last division of the 'Atlantic Coast Express' to Salisbury. The engine we were given was No. 34107 *Blandford Forum*, which had recently been fitted with ash pan dampers. She was still mainly in her original condition but we prepared the locomotive and went to Waterloo and hooked on to thirteen bogies. We left right time, and Charlie wielded the shovel in his best manner, but between Surbiton and Hampton Court Junction, Charlie looked at me, "I don't know what's wrong with her Bert" he said, indicating the boiler pressure gauge, which was showing 190. I leaned over and glanced in the fire, it was perfect, so I said, "Reverse the dampers, Charlie," which he did. He closed the back one and opened the front one. Immediately, the engine began to make steam and it was not long, only a few more miles further on, and she was 'standing around' just under the blowing off point of 250lbs with the injector working, and Charlie was happy once more. I believe he thought it was magic on my part, but after all, the engines were originally designed to work with no dampers at all. There was a gale of a wind going into the front of the ash pan which did not cause excessive fuel consumption, and when Charlie tried to use the back dampers she was just not getting enough air, so damper reversal alleviated the position. We were first stop Salisbury, arriving there right time and were relieved by Exeter men. On the return trip, we had No. 73118 which had come through from Exeter and the footplate was in the usual Exeter state of dust everywhere! It seemed that the coal hopper at Exmouth Junction pounded the Welsh coal into dust which proved most difficult to keep slaked down, the water simply running off the surface and away, instead of soaking into it. If one was able to get it really soaked, then it would be like mud, most difficult for firing and many a trip has been ruined because of this dust.

I sometimes sighed for the footplate cleanliness that the Yorkshire hard coals afforded. If the coal was slaked down it remained that way and all in all, hard coals were cleaner to work with despite the production of more smoke as compared with Welsh coal. I must say though, that the mechanical condition of the main line engines during this time was excellent and maintenance was good and the engines performed their work well, going through to Exeter and back in the same day. There had been a new rota for the 'Merchant Navys', designed to get maximum use from them and which was followed quite closely. For instance, the paper train engine was usually in the shed the previous day, that is for boiler wash-out, then the engine went 2.40am paper train to Bournemouth, back with the 7.20am then to Nine Elms for servicing, down with the 3pm to Exeter and back, I believe, with the Tavy goods to Nine Elms Goods Yard. She was then taken to Nine Elms about 4.30am for more servicing and then went down to Bournemouth with the 8.30am, the engine going through to Weymouth and back in the afternoon, arriving at Waterloo during the early evening. This was quite an extensive roster, and after about five days on this intensive work the fire was dropped and the brick arch and tube plate were cleaned down and the superheater flues blown out by the shed staff. It was a system that ensured that Nine Elms engines were kept to a good state and whenever a Bournemouth engine failed at Waterloo and a Nine Elms engine was substituted it was often several days before Bournemouth would relinquish the engine back to its own depot. This usually happened under pressure from Control or when the engine needed a heavy service because she was going 'off the boil' or was in need of a boiler wash-out.

The Exeter engines could always be relied upon to steam well as they were serviced regularly in the firebox every fifth day. As one fireman put it, referring to Exeter engines, "They are filthy but they go like a bomb", and he was correct!

On my return from annual leave, I was booked at 7.17am on Sunday, 6th September, to work the 9am to Salisbury. Charlie was my mate and we had No. 35020, the best of the rebuilt 'Merchant Navys'. We set off and had an excellent trip, but approaching Andover we must have been really moving, as I was applying the brake inside the distant signal and at the point where the road 'straightens up', one can see Andover station. I glanced at the ground and at the station, and thought, 'Blimey, we are not going to stop', so a full brake application was made and then the brake really held on this thirteen-coach train. As the train entered the platform, probably still doing 35 mph. I put the 'handle up' and began to blow off the brake and we came to a nice stand at the further end of the platform with half a coach just off the station ramp. It was a far better stop than I had thought possible a few moments before. One makes stops such as this very rarely in one's lifetime and it does not pay to make a habit of it, otherwise you'll find that the train does not stop at the required place. There is far more to stopping a train which is braked by the vacuum brake than appears at first sight. The brake is sluggish to go on and is more than sluggish to release when one has a long train.

About eight bogie coaches was considered the ideal length of train and the longer the train became then one had to be more careful with the application. *Bibby Line* was not fitted with a speedometer on this occasion and was a lively, buoyant locomotive with a deceptive speed capability. I guess I was somewhat lucky to have made such a good stop.

The following Thursday I was booked on my first Bournemouth turn, the 3.30pm 'down' in the afternoon. George Fursey was my fireman, now a driver at Euston. George was a good fireman, but he liked the boiler water well up in the glass whereas I was not too keen on that. It was possible with the free-steaming Bulleid boilers to get too much water in them and if one was a light engineman and not using quite the same amount of water, then that water would gradually creep up the glass well out of sight until the engine was on the verge of priming. It was a peculiar situation, as with a boiler full of water priming would take place if the safety valves were allowed to lift and this would happen when the injector was shut off. So I always maintained that water was best in sight in the glass and then if necessary the second injector could be put on in order to quieten it down. So, it was possible to do too well with the Bulleid boiler, and priming would result. Apart from the washing out of the cylinder lubricants, it would also have the dire consequences of knocking out the cylinder cover, which was a practice frowned upon by authority! Pressure relief valves on the front and back cylinder covers should release water if it is carried over, being set at a pound or two higher pressure than the boiler. Unhappily they seldom did so but would blow under dry superheat pressure.

During the teacher training course at Faverdale Hall, Darlington, I made many friends. We were all loco men from various parts of the country and it became known that there had never been a course quite like that of number 58. One of the chaps, a driver at Doncaster at the time, John Ross, said that he would like to have a ride on a Southern engine, so I suggested he obtain a footplate pass through his governor, and ride with me on the 9am to Salisbury one morning, which he did. On Monday, 28th September, I met John at Waterloo and he rode on the footplate of No. 35020 to Salisbury with us, my mate being John Pilcher. John Ross had a go at the firing on the 'down' trip as he was used to London & North Eastern Pacifics with wide fireboxes, and on the return trip with No. 30453, *King Arthur* himself, he had a go at the driving. All in all, it was a most pleasant day, and everyone enjoyed themselves. No footplate inspectors were present, as is usual when a guest is aboard, but as this particular guest was a loco man, he would know how to conduct himself on a footplate. John Ross became the Chief Footplate Inspector in the Doncaster area so he made good in the railway industry, but time marches on and he has now retired.

We had some excellent firemen at Nine Elms during this time. Bob Edwards, who never became a driver, leaving the industry, and Eddie Cooper, who emigrated to Australia. He was a good hard-working chap, although inclined to moan about various things. Usually the moaner got on with the job combining both in a satisfactory manner. Bill Ellery was another excellent chap, interested in his work and in mutual improvement classes. Some were enticed away from the railway with more lucrative jobs outside, whilst they enjoyed the work on steam engines, the lack of social activities was often a determining factor in their outlook, because after all, a young chap does need recreational activities.

These were my duties from Sunday 18th October on consecutive days: 3.02pm, 8.50pm, 8.50pm, 8.50pm, 8.50pm, 8.50pm, 6.05pm, Sunday again, 3.31pm, 1.35pm, 2.30pm, 2.30pm, 3.10pm and 2.30pm, on Friday 30th, and should have been late turn again on Saturday 31st, but I applied for leave because of the Faverdale reunion. Social turns of duty were few and far between on the loco rosters. The social time of duty was considered from about six o'clock in the morning until about ten. There were so many other duties with times which were away from these. 12.30am were early turns, 10.25pm were late turns and often these weeks would come together so that it was virtually a fortnight without a night in bed. One could be on duty at 11pm on a Saturday evening and again on duty at 12.01 Monday morning, and that was considered your Sunday off! Bearing in mind that booking on duty at 11pm Saturday night, your eight-hour day would be up at 7am on Sunday morning and one would need to spend the greater part of the day in bed in order to be fit to be up for duty at 1am or earlier on that Sunday night or early Monday morning.

On Tuesday 24th November 1959, a Top Link fireman, Jack Cambridge, was killed whilst on duty. He was looking for a distant signal whilst going through Eastleigh on the 'down' line when he was struck by a open door of a train standing on the 'up' through line. Jack's mate, Charlie 'Happy' Gordon, was very much distressed at this happening, and at the subsequent funeral on the Wednesday of the following week, a vast crowd of loco men, both from Nine Elms and Feltham attended a very moving ceremony. It was a sombre reminder that it is dangerous to put one's head out of the side of the cab too far and several years later, when I was working the 'down' paper train, the mate I had on that day was looking for the same distant signal and when he saw it at 'caution', he called to me – "It's on". I made a full application of the brake and over-ran 'Stoneham Intermediate' by 150 yards! So, a few seconds saved by putting one's head too far out could result in stopping at the signal in question or, as fate would have it, on Jack's day, he was struck by an open door. I hasten to add, the 'Stoneham distant' was visible from the right hand side of the engine several seconds earlier, and I was sharply reminded during my own incident of Jack's efforts several years previously. February 1966 was the date of my 'run by'.

I was still in the market for a change-over of duties and one turn for which I used to change, although it was not initiated by me, although I was willing to do so, was on a Sunday. There were twelve turns in my link and twelve turns in No. 1 link. In my own link we had the 2.54pm to Basingstoke, booking on duty at 1.15pm, rather early for dinner, but it was a nice little turn and one would finish around about 8.30pm or 9pm. 'Happy' Gordon's duty was the six o'clock to Salisbury and back with the milk, and as he lived at Wimbledon, he found it difficult to get home. This was the latest time that No. 1 link booked on and it came once every twelve weeks, but 'Happy' and I found it quite mutual to change over on these Sundays. He would do my 2.54pm to Basingstoke and return and I would do the six o'clock to Salisbury and back with the milk. It was quite convenient for me as I only lived twelve minutes walk from the depot, and my wife also appreciated not having to prepare a Sunday lunch for abut 12.30pm, two hours later being the norm.

On one occasion on this duty we were late off the shed because the preparing driver had some difficulties, and consequently we left Waterloo about five minutes late. My mate was Reg Knight and our train was only nine coaches, so I asked him, "By milepost 31 in even time Reg?" "All right by me", he replied. So I 'pushed' No. 35009 *Shaw Savill* a little more than need be, after observing the permanent speed restrictions out to Surbiton. She began to 'fly' – easy work really as Reg was not at all distressed, green lights all the way as traffic was sparse on Sunday evenings. No. 35009 sailed past milepost 31 in Purbright Cutting comfortably inside 31 minutes and now I had to ease her, otherwise we would have been in Basingstoke well inside the 55 minute allowance and I would have earnt myself a reputation as a speed merchant! Even so, we stopped there in 48 minutes from Waterloo, regaining in full the late start, plus another couple of minutes. Such times are nothing today with powerful diesel and electric stock, but on a steam engine the power has to be generated by the fireman, and upon him depends the quality of a trip.

Other turns came my way such as the 5.39pm to Salisbury, which I did for Sid Bracher and he did my mid-day turn, or whatever I had. Sid lived at Raynes Park and he also found it difficult to get home without wasting a lot of time waiting for trains during the small hours.

Likewise, on the early shift, I was approached by Frank Saunders, when I had three trips to Salisbury on the nine o'clock. He asked me if I would care to do his paper train in lieu, so, always looking for a better job, I was happy to oblige, and I enjoyed the trips on the paper train, despite the starting time of 1.45am. The most difficult thing on such duties was getting the necessary sleep so I made myself stay up until about tea-time then went to bed, just about fagged out, sleeping until about 12.30am when it was time to get up. It was absolutely essential on such duties to get adequate rest as there was nothing worse than being in charge of a main line train and feeling drowsy. This position became far worse in later years with the introduction of the diesel and diesel electric locomotives with which to work these trains. The steam locomotive itself is not conducive to making one feel drowsy, such as the close confines of a diesel cab. Frank Saunders was our Branch Secretary at the time and was failing in health, and a time on duty of 8.20am was far more beneficial to him than 1.45am, so, in that respect, I was happy to be able to help Frank.

Troubles with a 'Lord Nelson'

On Sunday 14th February 1960, I was booked on duty at 5.59pm to work the 7.30pm to Bournemouth as far as Eastleigh. The engine we were given was No. 30854 *Howard of Effingham*, and my mate was Brian Mercer. The fire looked quite dirty at Nine Elms so Brian luffed out some of the dirt in the absence of any assisting fireman and we had to make the best of it. We went out and filled up the tender with coal and water, and then made our way up to Waterloo and left right time, boiler filled right up and near to blowing off. Going by Hampton Court Junction we were back on about 150psi and half a glass of water. It was dark and I asked Brian, "Are you familiar with the road?", and he replied, that he was. So I then said, "Right, come over here and let me see what I can do with her". I removed my serge jacket and stowed it away, borrowed Brian's gloves, then took the shovel and held it in the firehole in such a manner that I could peer up the length of the long fire-box to see the condition of the fire. It was not burning fiercely enough so I took the pricker from the tender, fortunately long enough to reach seven or eight feet of the fire (the grate of a 'Lord Nelson' is 10ft 6in long) and gave the fire a good 'rux-up'. The back damper was about two-thirds open, enough to give good passage of the primary air flow up through the grate. The front damper remained closed and I pulled the firehole sliding doors nearly shut and dropped the short bar over to keep the doors apart by two inches. The top flap was dropped down also, and now I watched the chimney for the occasional spark. The boiler pressure gauge had stopped its backward slide, the reverser was set on 20 per cent cut-off and the main valve of the regulator was just 'broken'. The driver's side injector was feeding water into the boiler steadily, as sometimes the exhaust injector on the fireman's side could not be adjusted 'fine enough', so very desirable on an ailing engine on a fairly long non-stop run. We had a second class Welsh coal on the tender and I sighed for some good quality hard Yorkshire coal with its almost instant heat. Anyway the fire had brightened up considerably as it burned down and we were getting some degree of superheat. Firing now commenced, little and often with never a full shovelful of coal as it is more easily directed to where it is required.

The engine was making her own speed over the slight 'ups and downs' to Woking, and I was watching the signals, hoping that we would get a distant at 'caution' so that the regulator could be closed and permit a lit-tle 'blow up'. However, as usual under the circumstances, we had green lights all the way, although a check through Woking would not have been favourable in view of the long drag up through Brookwood to milepost

31. Once over the top the regulator was opened wide, closed and re-opened on to the 'first valve'. The water in the gauge glass still showed just under half a glass, the boiler had rallied slightly and we had not reached the stage where it was necessary to shut off the steam heat to the train – mind you, it was not on at the full 50psi as demanded by the Appendix to the W.T.T., but about 30psi was going through the apparatus. We were steadily losing time, probably running at 10 to 15mph below the speed required to time the train, but at least we kept going. *Howard of Effingham* was responding, albeit sluggishly, to my administrations and when Brian closed the regulator – in good time for the Basingstoke stop – I started the exhaust injector in order to get some more water into the boiler, thus making full use of the short respite. We left Basingstoke with 170psi on the clock and two-thirds of a glass of water. I shut off both injectors as Brian got the 'Nelson' under way again, about 20 minutes 'down'.

As the fire brightened up under the second valve, working up to Worting Junction I restarted the left hand side injector and plied the shovel in the time-honoured LSWR tradition, systematically around the box, never two shovelfuls in the same place, 'light, tight and bright', to produce superheating for more economical working of the locomotive. The top of the bank is in Roundwood Tunnel and now we had eleven miles of downhill running to favour us. The regulator was placed on to the first valve and '854 began to get a move on, on the falling gradient through Micheldever and to Winchester, our next station stop. As at Basingstoke, as soon as the regulator was closed I started the exhaust injector, and as the coal watering hose was operable from that boiler feed, I was able to give the footplate a wash down and slake the coal on the tender. At this juncture a porter came up to the footplate, "Control wants to know if you require another engine", he announced. I was somewhat surprised, as it was most unusual for 'Control' to make such a move, because usually it was up to the driver to request another engine or assisting engine. It had not occurred to me to make such a move as the hardest part of our trip was over and we were winning the battle with the boiler. I answered the porter, "No, she will go through to Bournemouth", and at that moment I had every confidence that I would get '854 there if our relief did not show up at Eastleigh! So, we left Winchester with a respectable 190psi, and water one inch down the long gauge glass, the blower was now making itself felt as, when the boiler pressure is down on Lemaitre blastpipe fitted engines, the blower is not too effective.

When our relief stepped aboard at Eastleigh, 24 minutes late, the 'old girl', had 200psi on the clock and the water was bobbing in and out of the top nut on the gauge frame. The fire was thin and incandescent, certainly not a thick, heavy one, and here I must say, the 'Nelsons' were not any-one's engine. They required handling from both sides of the footplate to get the best results and were a hard taskmaster for an inexperienced fireman. They also did not respond to a thrashing as would a 'King Arthur', or the BR Standard Class 5s – sensitive handling brought forth its own response and to an engineman, they were superb engines, a delight to ride, and work upon.

Brian and I gathered our belongings, explained away our late running to the Eastleigh crew and walked down to the shed where, after our P.N. break, we were to prepare another engine to work some vans and empty stock to Waterloo for Monday morning's 'paper train'. A can of tea was made and we sat in the enginemens' mess room. Some 20 minutes after leaving *Howard of Effingham*'s footplate, the Running Shift Foreman came in, looked around and said to me, "You down with the 7.30pm?" I answered in the affirmative. "Well driver," he said, "My man is at Southampton and has asked for anther engine!" "What's his trouble?", I asked. "Short of steam", was the reply. I shrugged, "We had our troubles, but we got her here, even if we were late, and your chap does eight miles and wants another engine!" The Supervisor gave me a quizzical look and departed, but in defence of the Eastleigh crew, I should add that they may have had a boiler tube begin to leak, although there was no mention of that in my conversation with the Foreman.

Leaking tubes and a dirty fire would need a deal of overcoming as bad leaks tend to extinguish the fire! The 'Nelsons' failed more often with the boiler than with mechanical defects. During the war it was not unknown for Nine Elms' men to work to Bournemouth on one, have an excellent trip and of necessity, allow the fire to become dull and lose heat, then have boiler tubes begin to leak and either request a main line engine or take on a pilot, usually a T9, or a "U Boat" for the return trip. This was subject to availability on the part of the Bournemouth C. Running Foreman; a big engine or a small one with the crew and necessary road knowledge.

Regular Firemen

Progress for firemen through the links was more rapid than that of drivers, partly because the senior firemen were passed to act as drivers or went away from the depot on appointment as drivers at electric train depots, or merely left the service. After Charlie, I had John Burt, a chap keen on railways, which stemmed from his father, himself a railwayman. I got on well with John during the few weeks he was with me, but when he finally reached the Top Link he had an altercation with his driver, Ern Harvey, and in a fit of pique, he submitted his resignation. Subsequently he joined the LTE and became a driver on the District Line. I kept in touch with him and knew he always regretted leaving Nine Elms. On his journeys in and out of Wimbledon LTE terminus he would look with envy when a main line steam-hauled train went by. Through ill health, John left London Transport and went to live in Bognor, where my wife and I visited him on occasion and it was a shock to learn that he had passed away on 15th September 1986.

After John had gone up into 3A link, I obtained the services of Les Hoath, a chap about as fat as two bean poles! How he found the strength to fire big engines, I shall never know, but he managed, and managed well. One night we were bringing a "Black Motor", an LSWR Class 700 0-6-0 freight engine from the Goods Yard to Nine Elms Loco, and as we came through the Skew Arch between North and South Viaduct boxes, he said "Dummy's (ground signal) off Bert." That signal was at the further end of the Engine Line, controlled from Loco Junction box, and I knew exactly where to look but could not see it until we had travelled for maybe a couple of engine lengths and, at that moment, I realised my eyesight had begun to wane.

On Saturday, 30th July 1960, Les and I were rostered to sign on duty at 9.55am for the 10.10am off the shed, (engine prepared) for an early portion of the 'A.C.E.', 10.45am to Salisbury. I was waiting on the engine, No. 34009 *Lyme Regis*, outside the R/F's office when out he came, "Bert Hulbert, the Galloping Major". He called up to me, "Your mate's not here". I replied, "I know that, we'd have been on our way by now." The supervisor went on, "I've only got a young chap called Steyn." "If he is the only chap you've got, you'd best send him out" I rejoined. He disappeared and within a few moments a stocky young chap appeared carrying a teacan. I thought, 'Well, that's a good sign'. He climbed aboard. "Been to Salisbury?" I asked and he replied that he had not. I blew up for the exit signal and we were soon on our way to Waterloo. I watched the lad couple up and transfer the headcode from the tender to the front of the engine (top and bottom for the main line to Salisbury and beyond), and check the smokebox door was tight.

Regaining the footplate, young Jock had poured out the tea, but before drinking it I checked the fire, and as we had Welsh coal I added some around the sides and back corners without making any smoke. The boiler was topped up and the footplate washed down. Promptly, at 10.45 we got the 'right away' signal and No. 34009 got her eleven coaches into motion. As we approached Vauxhall the safety valves were about to lift. "Put the feed on mate", I called out. Steyn started the injector and promptly sat down again. Down past Nine Elms Loco and Queens Road we sailed, and after West London Junction, I eased the regulator to 20psi in the steam chest and put on the blower, ready for the 40 mph slack through Clapham Junction. Halfway through the platform, I called to Steyn, "Shut off the injector", and as I re-opened the regulator to get the train into speed again, he sat down once more. I went on – "Come on, get stuck in, don't be afraid of her". He looked at me with some astonishment, "What, already" he answered. "Put the shovel round this way", I said and a quick glance at the road ahead and I added coal to the fire, another look ahead, more coal on to the fire, and the boiler responded. I went across the footplate and started the injector, cutting it fine so as to avoid wasting water, which happens everytime an injector is put on and shut off. "Look Jock, I'm not doing it all, you have a go. Just drop it in the door and try to get some in the back corners," I instructed. He was willing but obviously inexperienced. A moving locomotive is not exactly a stable platform for coal heaving, particularly so as it has to be directed to its proper place in the firebox, whilst the amount of heat which comes back at one through an open firehole door is sometimes overbearing. A good baffleplate in the firehole keeps the heat where it is most effective, but the Bulleid Pacifics were not so fitted in their original condition, but instead there was the steam operated Ajax firehole doors, operated by a foot treadle. A splendid arrangement when the apparatus was adjusted properly by the fireman, somewhat noisy – especially when too much steam was admitted, causing the doors to fly open when the treadle was depressed, with enough force to nearly lift the copious oil admissary boxes off the boiler backhead! If the treadle was released too early there was the risk of trapping one's wrists in the doors along with the shovel – but that was only done once! So, this apparatus became abused, and the vast majority of firemen would leave the doors open all the time firing was in progress, with the foot pedal tucked out of the way, then nearly closing the doors when the current round of firing was completed. Without use and lubrication the Ajax doors fell into disuse. On No. 34009 this was the order of things and I would watch where Jock was putting the coal in the firebox, and then add my quota when I deemed it necessary.

After passing Hampton Court Junction we were finished with continuous colour light signalling, and the signal sections became more spaced out and so I was able to devote a little more attention to the demands of the boiler. In fact, I rather enjoyed the experience as I thought of my main line firing days when it was possible to maintain the boiler to my driver's satisfaction, and to see every signal en route. In addition I was sharply reminded of my father's words when the examination to act as a driver was passed. "When you sign the route card you undertake to do both jobs." Meaning, if you aspire to run trains you have to be prepared to help young and inexperienced mates, and this was brought home to me in full measure that Saturday morning on the first portion of the 'A.C.E.' Had I been ten minutes late at Salisbury then all the several portions of that famous train would undoubtedly have suffered also! Suffice to say we arrived at the Cathedral City in exactly the 90 minutes allowed, followed by the usual six minute flurry at the water column. My mate held the 'bag' in the tender, and the relieving fireman attended to the boiler and checked his fire. I put a drop of oil in the piston gland cups and slidebars, feeling the bearings as I went along the sides, whilst my relief stood ready to turn off the water when the tender was filled. Salisbury MPD usually turned out two cleaners to shovel some coal forward on the tenders during the stop, witnessed by the usual throng of railway enthusiasts.

After some much needed refreshments, we relieved the crew on one of Mr Urie's S15 mixed traffic 4-6-0 tender engines, No. 30512, to work a 'stopper', all stations to Woking. This was a turn on which the S15s rarely found employment in the '60s. No. 30512 had seen better days, and I had come to that conclusion before we entered Fisherton Tunnel! There was the usual thump and bang from the big ends and axleboxes, along with the peculiar mincing motion the locos had when they were 'run down'. I instructed Jock to keep the fire well up at the back end, not to black out the fire at the front of the grate and when he was firing there, keep the handle of the shovel up otherwise the coal would strike the brick arch and fall short. I checked the hydrostatic lubricator was working satisfactorily and demonstrated to my mate how to use the shovel on a longish firegrate. He responded well and between us we 'made ends meet'. The worst section of that trip was the last, from Woking to Waterloo when No. 30512 was pushed into somewhat unaccustomed speed! At least under those circumstances the fire works down the grate and one has only to feed the sides and keep it well up 'under the door'. Another concern on a rough engine is that the injector water feeds have an occasional disarming desire to either work open or closed when running hard, usually exactly opposite to what is required at that particular moment in time.

I had had a lesson in that particular area when I was firing during the war. I was with Sam Hardy on one of the Salisbury 'Arthurs', and running up through Wimbledon the exhaust injector began to spit and splutter. I turned it off and went across the footplate to start the driver's side live steam injector, only to find the water feed valve wide open and the tender tank was empty. Fortunately, there was sufficient water in the boiler to get us into Waterloo, so Sam suddenly became an economical engineman as we did not want to have to stop to throw out the fire, or either go into Clapham Junction Loop, come off the train and go into the yard to obtain some of the precious fluid. Driver George Diddems always maintained that three quarters of a glass of water at Wimbledon would be sufficient to get into the Terminus and on this occasion he was proved correct (always provided there were no heavy delays over the final miles!) What a relief it was to hear water gurgle into the tank as soon as uncoupling was finished and the tender had been positioned by the adjacent water column near the buffer stops at Waterloo station. It was several days later I saw my mate Les Hoath, and true to his nature, he thought that 'dropping it' on that Saturday – not deliberately I hasten to add – was a huge joke!

Out of Gauge Load to Cobham

On the week of Monday 28th November 1960, my rostered turn was 'down' with the 7.54pm to Basingstoke and back with the 'Sidmouth Milk'. On the Wednesday the roster clerk left me a note stating, very regretfully, that he would have to remove me from my rostered job on the Friday evening as I was the only driver available with the necessary route knowledge to cover a 'special' from Stewarts Lane to Cobham, on the Guildford 'New Line'. I was put back to 9.45pm and my mate was Brian Robery. I obtained my 'stencil' for the job, which indicated the train consisted of a well wagon with a brake van at each end, conveying an out of gauge steel bridge for replacing a time elapsed structure at Cobham. We were given a Standard Class 4, 4-6-0 tender engine and the job proved most interesting. As the load was out of gauge it meant that we could not pass any traffic on the opposite line, and between Wimbledon and Hampton Court Junction we were booked to travel on the local line – Wimbledon A to Wimbledon C, on the through, then on to the local line. During this time we were not to be overtaken by traffic running on the fast line. Speed was to be 15 mph and as the loco was fitted with an accurate speedometer is was relatively simple to keep to the nominated speed. However, I quickly found that the heavy load was very free running on down gradients, yet a change to upwards soon caused the engine to slow very quickly with consequent, and frequent adjustment of the regulator. I must confess that I did not realise there were so many *minor* gradient changes between Stewarts Lane and Cobham! Heavy gradients, such as climbing out of Stewarts Lane to Latchmere Junction and then up to Clapham Junction A box, followed by the sharp climb from Point Pleasant up to East Putney were readily accounted for, but as soon as the gradient changed – wow! – that heavily laden well wagon really pushed up against the tender. This caused me to apply the steam brake in varying degrees of pressure; the brake arrangements on the Standards was first class as the application handle was on a ratchet and could be set to any desired place, from just rubbing the blocks on to the wheels to a full application. The business of removing a driver from his rostered turn of duty to cover the work when there was not a 'spare man' available with the necessary route knowledge was accepted, as it did keep work at the depot, something that was always jealously guarded. The roster clerk would be loathe to turn work away and would only do so if he was unable to cover it. Often men would be borrowed from other depots during busy periods, especially the firemen, and in the case of Jock Steyn, previously related, he may well have been on loan from another depot, such as Feltham or Guildford, as I had not seen him previously and did not do so again!

Promotion to No. 3A Link
On Monday 20th February 1961 I gained promotion to No. 3A Link, at one time known as the 'Tavy Gang'. Although the work therein had very little resemblance to that which prevailed in the link prior to the war when most of the jobs were 'double home' i e signing off at Exeter or Dorchester. The fireman whom I joined was Terry Regan, and we were rostered on duty at 8.50pm to prepare a Pacific and work the 10.35pm 'Tavy', an express freight train, from Nine Elms Goods to Salisbury. BoB No. 34081 *92 Squadron*, was the loco allocated and with only about 38 wagons (mostly fitted) the Bulleid loco, in its original condition, made

light work of the job. Watching Terry at work with the shovel caused me to think that I had 'struck lucky' in having a responsible chap for my mate. The return trip from Salisbury was another fitted freight, a 'Market' train, meaning it was loaded with perishables for Covent Garden. The train rolled in from Exeter with an S15, No. 30830, on the front. The Pacific, which should have been there, had failed (a rare occurrence) and my first thoughts were that it was going to be a dusty trip, something which I hated. However, the S15 was in reasonable condition, the drawgear was up tight so the tender did not endeavour to run faster than the engine, which usually brought the coal forward in unwanted quantities and accompanied by vast clouds of coal dust, the coal watering hose being somewhat ineffective under those circumstances. So, Terry was able to keep the coal well watered and No. 30830 was master of the 40 wagons or so of the 'Up Market'.

Up the bank to Porton 35 per cent cut-off and a touch of the big regulator was sufficient to time the train, and once over the top at Grateley the regulator was put back on to the first port and then gradually eased until the pistons were just 'floating'. Once the distant signal for Redpost Junction was sighted in the clear position the regulator was opened out onto the first full port in order to keep the engine speed up and pull the train through the dip by the Junction box, thus keeping the couplings stretched out and avoiding a 'snatch'. Over the small brow, and with Andover outer distant 'off', the loco was kept going through the station, on a falling gradient, the speed probably reaching 55 to 60 mph. When Enham Intermediate distant was sighted and passed, the big regulator was opened and with 30 per cent cut-off and the ensuing gradient was tackled in good style to MP $62^1/_2$. Down the following mile of 1 in 275 with controls unchanged but nearing the bottom of the incline, I advanced the cut-off by one nick on the reverser ($2^1/_2$ per cent) to keep up the engine speed, up through Hurstbourne (now demolished) and once through Whitchurch the gradient eased and the cut-off was reduced to 30 per cent. Approaching Oakley at MP 54, the regulator was opened wide, then closed and reopened immediately on to the first valve. We were roughly on the same level as St Pauls and the harder work on the part of the engine – and my mate, was now finished, as it was mostly gentle gradients, almost all in our favour, all the way to Nine Elms Goods and No. 30830 made light work of the job. One thing I noticed though on that trip was, how cold it was, at least for me, with those open fronted tenders after the cosy confines of a Bulleid Pacific's cab!

Fireman Tom McArthur
Terry did not stay with me many weeks, as he was 'shunted' up into No. 2 Link and Tom McArthur took his place. Tom was a big man and a most likeable one. Our first real main line turn was on the Tuesday following Easter Monday, 4th April, 1961, on the 8.35am from Waterloo to

Bournemouth. Having signed on at Vauxhall Time Office, we went 'pass' to the Terminus to find a WC No. 34103 *Calstock* on the front of the train. The crew whom we relieved soon departed which gave us a few moments to 'take stock'. I checked that we had a full brake reading of 21in of vacuum showing on the gauge, then down to the train to see if the first coach or two brake pistons were fully 'down'. If not, I would have pulled the strings until the piston dropped. Alternatively, I could have put my foot against the brake blocks and if they moved then the brake was 'off', and if not, ie, the brake blocks were on the wheel rims, I would have had to have gone down the whole train and 'pull the strings'. It is always possible that the engine which brought the empty stock into Waterloo had created 22in of vacuum in the train, which, unless correct- ed, as I was wont to do, would have meant dragging brakes on the outgo- ing service. The rubbing brake blocks would then get warm and expand, causing a tighter grip on the wheels until the driver was forced to stop the train and take remedial action! There was an answer to the problem though and that was to place some wet paper around the 'pepper box' and thus increase its vacuum limiting capabilities. The vacuum gauge needle may rise to 23in or 24in of brake and the brake on the train would release, but if the engine was changed en route, the strings would have to be pulled to release the excess vacuum on the chamber side of the apparatus, usually a time consuming chore, and if a shunter was around then he would be asked to do it.

Calstock was in her original condition, air smoothed, with chain driven valve gear in an oil bath, steam reverser, etc., and was in 'good nick'. I was really enjoying life, a good engine, a good mate and nice running weather, clear and mild. *Calstock* was running as only a true Bulleid Pacific can, quiet, smooth, effortless, the steam reverser 'holding up' well – what more could a man want? We called at Surbiton, Woking and Basingstoke and as we were running into Micheldever, regulator closed of course, Tom elected to pick up the shovel and added coal to the fire! Whilst I was looking back for the guard's tip to restart the train, the fol- lowing conversation took place. "Tom, are you aware that what you have just done is the height of bad firing?" "What's that Bert?" "Putting some on when running into a station, making unnecessary smoke. Some of the old drivers would have kicked that shovel out of your hands!" Tom replied, "I didn't know that. No other driver has ever told me so, I wish you would tell me more as I want to learn."

The guard was waving his flag and I set No. 34103 into motion down the bank to Winchester, the advance starter was sighted and passed. I motioned to Tom to 'catch' the distant signal for Weston box, he did so and now I answered Tom's last remarks. "Right then mate. If you want to learn we will have any rule or engine subject you desire whenever you feel like it, and on the road, I'll prompt you on the do's and don'ts of making our job a 'snip' and a pleasure." So began an interesting period for us both and Tom rapidly became a 'good mate', blowing off steam and smoke making was kept to a minimum, our footplate was kept generally clear of coal and dust and economy in all things relating to footplate work was reached. On that particular job we were relieved at Bournemouth Central and were not required for work until we relieved on an 'up' service at 1.15pm, so there were two hours for a leisurely meal break etc., which included Tom's first 'mutual improvement class' session on his quest for knowledge.

The return trip was a 'doddle', BoB class 4-6-2 Pacific No. 34087 *145 Squadron*, was our charge, and which had been modified at Eastleigh Works less than five months previously. The load was a comparatively light one of nine coaches and a bogie van, about 340 tons, and with a 'Battle of Britain', in good nick, there was no need to extend the loco or the fireman. Useless to 'chase her along' and then have to wait for time at the stations; different if there had been a delay of some description, then there was justification to recoup the lost time. (But some drivers I have known would not make up a minute if the train was running late due to signal or PW slacks or even overtime at the stations!) I guess that some writers in the popular railway press would describe that as unenterprising running. Maybe so, but seldom, if ever, is praise given to the thousands of drivers who timed their trains correctly through each section with the minimum expenditure of coal and water. But, let us get back to Tom McArthur and *145 Squadron*. Whilst we were standing at Woking awaiting the 'right away' for the last lap to Waterloo, Tom asked me, "How did you use to run them into Waterloo?" I replied, "I'll show you, put the shovel this way Tom." He did so, and after getting No. 34087 on the move again, checking the signals ahead (Maybury Intermediate) I looked into the firebox. My mate had a reasonable fire, almost level with the firehole ring and sloping nicely to the front and sides, and if we had the same amount of fire in the box at Clapham Junction our relief would have been quick to ask, "Don't you know where Waterloo is yet?", as, apart from the difficulty of keeping the engine quiet at the terminus during the 20 minutes or so standing on the stop blocks awaiting the departure of the empty stock, there would have been the avoidable hard work on the part of the fireman in dealing with the fire on disposal at Nine Elms mpd. With this in mind, the aim was to come to rest at Waterloo with about 200psi of steam, half a glass of water in the boiler and a low fire down one side of the firegrate.

After a judicious prod on the fire with the shovel on the left side, I commenced to run down the fire on that side whilst firing more heavily on the right hand side. Once past Surbiton the demands on the boiler lessened and between New Malden and Raynes Park I said to Tom, "That will do us now, barring any delays." The road was clear into Waterloo, arriving there at 4.09pm, right time, Tom had washed down the footplate, with hot water ready in the bucket for hand washing and the required boiler control had been attained. The fire was virtually out on the left side of the grate whilst an adequate amount of well burnt through fire lay on the opposite side, all accomplished without using any fire irons! All the relieving fireman needed to do was run the dart down the low fire side, which would effectively burn any cinders on the way to Nine Elms, and on arrival there the hoppers would be opened. The fire-bars would then be shaken and opened to the dumping position, the broken up clinker and dirt would fall into the pit via the hopper, and the firebars repositioned ready for the fire to be transferred from the right side to the clean side, exposing the clinker and dirt, then the process would be repeated. Tom expressed his surprise that 'running in a fire' to Waterloo could be done in such an apparently casual manner. "You have to plan ahead mate" I answered, "Always remember you can put a bit on but you can't take it off and in the future, if you feel you have overdone the fire, then tell me at Esher. It's no use asking me to get rid of some fire at Clapham Junction – it's too late then." I did not entirely approve of the practice of 'dropping her over', meaning advancing the cut-off to produce a heavier blast upon the fire for a few miles in order to burn away the excess fire, but at least it saved 'red faces' and apologies, as well as eliminating the problem mentioned previously on arrival at journey's end. It was all 'part and parcel' of how enginemen could, and did, help one another with a little forethought on the immediate job in hand. On the other hand, it was possible to run into Waterloo with the fire too low, necessitating adding coal whilst under the station roof, a practice not encouraged by officialdom because of the smoke nuisance, together with the fact that the fireman would be dealing with a partly 'green fire' on arrival at Nine Elms. This made it more difficult to see what he was doing in the firebox, especially with hard (long flame) coals on the tender.

Tom McArthur was with me for a few short weeks only. He was an apt pupil but when he took a turn 'on the regulator' on one occasion, I needed to reproach him on his handling of the engine as he was hustling the 'old girl' along as though an automatic stoker was supplying the firebox with fuel! I called out to him, "Oi, ease your hand Tom, I'm 50 not 30!" He was most apologetic, "I didn't want to lose any time Bert", he answered. "Pull the lever up to 25 per cent and ease the regulator" I instructed and Tom did so. "That's better. You won't lose time mate, but if you do, I'll answer for it." So Tom settled down to enjoy the driving whilst I was happy to supply the hot steam necessary to keep time. After that he became more used to my methods, and I considered that ultimately he would become an efficient engineman. Promotion through the links was rapid for Tom. He passed the examination for driving duties in a good manner and began to get booked out driving on the menial jobs, but, on 14th September 1964, he was tragically killed whilst running BR Standard Class 5, No. 73065, tender first from Wimbledon West Yard, light engine, to Nine Elms Loco. On approaching Clapham Junction, Tom put his head out of the cab to 'spot' a colour light signal and he struck the buttress of a bridge, which killed him instantly. His young fireman of the day stopped the engine in the platform and sought the necessary assistance. He was so upset that he left the railway service whilst the rest of us at Nine Elms mourned the passing of a fine and popular man. Indeed, one and all were reminded of the dangers which existed in our calling, and still do as witness the terrible accident at Clapham Junction on 12th December 1988, within a stone's throw of where Tom lost his life some 24 years earlier.

Winston Churchill Causes Some Problems

One day, I had a fireman named Eddie Cooper, a real moaner, but at the same time a hard worker, and a good chap with 'the blade'. We had gone down to Salisbury on the 3pm from Waterloo to Exeter on MN No. 35014 *Nederland Line*, having a normal trip. We were booked back on the 6.33pm 'up' from the Cathedral City, and awaiting the train's arrival, it came in with BoB No. 34051 *Winston Churchill* on the front, emitting horrible groaning noises from the front end! As soon as the pipe was in the tender and the water was flowing in I hastened to the front of the engine to check the mechanical lubricators, of which there were three in line, sealed and fed from a common tank. I removed the filler cap expecting the oil level therein to be well down, but it wasn't, so I tried the actuating rod, which was attached to a valve rocker. There was a lot of slack on it which meant that when the engine was notched up and the valve travel shortened, the lubricator rods did not get enough 'throw' to turn the pumps! I gave the hand ratchet wheels as many turns as time would allow in order to pump some oil into the valves and pistons, hoping to stop the 'old girl' groaning. Station work completed, the tender filled, a green flag from the guard and we were on our way.

The oil that I had pumped in by hand now settled onto the dry surfaces, and was blown around by the steam, and to my relief the groaning subsided. I did not 'pull her up' inside 45 per cent cut-off and used the regulator to judge the power output, thus making sure the piston valve travel was long enough to ensure the lubricator actuating rods had sufficient movement on them to work the pumps. On reaching the top of the bank just before Grateley I closed the regulator and put the reverser into full forward gear to get maximum travel on the valve etc. Then, to my amazement Eddie had the pricker in the fire and was hauling several large lumps of clinker out of the fire and onto the footplate. Needless to say my mate lived up to his reputation, whilst the language was quite 'picturesque' belabouring in a verbal manner the shortcomings of the Exmouth Junction fireman who had done the disposal work on *Winston Churchill*! Hooking clinker from the fire of a loco fitted with a steel firebox was not advisable with the regulator open, so Eddie made the most of the time available whilst coasting down the gradient from Grateley to Andover Junction. No. 34051 was running more sweetly now, obviously getting the desired lubrication in the 'front end' and my mate having fettled up the fire to his satisfaction. Thereafter, we had a more normal trip, plenty of lever and a narrow regulator opening. Time was not lost thanks to the remarkable free running of the Bulleid Pacifics and Eddie was not called upon to work too hard with the shovel.

Before they were rebuilt those Pacifics were the only express engines that I have known whereby it was possible to close the regulator at speed and put the valve gear into full forward travel without any noticeable effect on the running qualities or noise level of the engine. They just 'sailed' quietly along, in sharp contrast to the conventional piston valve locomotive. In fact, on the latter, I would keep a breath of steam 'on' until coming to a stand or alternatively, on closing the regulator, I would pull the lever more towards midgear so as to provide compression in the cylinders to allay the big-end knock. There would be a retarding effect upon the engine but I thought it was more desirable than having the big-ends flaying around with all the accompanying noise. So, having arrived at Nine Elms Loco with No. 34051 and obtained relief by a disposal crew, I booked the lubricator actuating rods slack, which would be given attention and rectified, before the engine was booked out on her next job.

I recently asked Ted Benn, whom I knew as a fitter at Nine Elms, what was the cause of the actuating rods becoming slack. He explained that it was usually the supporting bracket bolts working loose ($\frac{1}{2}$in bolts) and was normally a simple job to remedy.

Going back to Eddie Cooper, within a few months of being booked with me on that day he left the railway and emigrated to Australia, taking his family with him. However the story filtered back to Nine Elms that he lost his young son of several months on the long sea voyage. I hasten to add, that I do not think his decision to emigrate was the result of being booked with me on only one occasion! I have sometimes wondered if he found employment on Australian Railways, if not on the footplate, because he was getting on a bit to start engine cleaning, then firing, etc., assuming the Aussie promotion was similar to that which prevailed here, ie, strict seniority; or became a railwayman in other grades. As far as I am aware, he did not correspond with any of his former colleagues at the Premier Depot.

Southampton Boat Trains

Air travel as we know it today was not so prevalent in the early sixties and folk still travelled by ocean liner, so there were boat trains to and fro between Waterloo and Southampton Docks, some on a rostered basis on Thursdays, but mostly as Specials. Nine Elms men usually worked the 'down' trains with any suitable available engine, whilst the coaching stock was provided by Clapham Yard, where the shunters would be booked to work extra time to make up the boat trains. Sometimes they had Pullman cars in them, but invariably with a dining car in the consist. According to traffic requirements, the stock would sometimes be worked back empty to Clapham Yard, but if not, the engine would be taken light to Eastleigh mpd for stabling, then home 'smoker' on the first available train to Waterloo. I once worked a boat train of 13 coaches into the Old Docks, a nightmare of a place with roads and lines running in all directions, at 12 noon, just as all the dock workers were streaming out for the lunch break. The shunter/pilotman was unable to stop the flow of road traffic so I was forced to stop, which was most undesirable as the train was on an 'S' curve with the rear still fouling Canute Road Crossing (the main road). When I did get the tip to restart, the engine, a rebuilt WC would not move either way! Fortunately one of the new 600 hp 0-6-0 diesel shunting engines was on hand, and the shunter pulled a pair of points and called him back onto the front of the WC. A three-link coupling was thrown over our coupling hook, the diesel engine was reversed and the power controller opened – and to my surprise the whole train was moved with consummate ease and I did not need to open the regulator. Needless to say, I was somewhat relieved that our predicament did not last too long and our red faces were short lived. So, within the confines of the Docks it was imperative to keep a heavy train moving, thus the shunter/pilotman would leap off the front steps of the engine and run to set a pair of points or stop road traffic on the intersection. (A train had priority over the latter.) Usually though, when one entered the Docks with a passenger train, there was a flagman, normally recruited from the platelayers, on every set of facing points as there were no ground signals or facing point locks to indicate to the driver that the points would not move under his engine.

When I was firing I was booked with George Hawkins on one of the very first boat trains to run from Waterloo to Southampton Docks after the war, probably 1945. Our engine was No. 772 *Sir Brian* a 'King Arthur' class 4-6-0 and the load was 16 vehicles, including nine Pullman cars – a hefty load for a two-cylinder engine. I experienced a thrill on that day which was rekindled on almost every occasion when I was booked on a boat train, even with diesel traction. There was always something indefinable, an aura abut the words 'Boat Train', a legacy I guess from steam engines and ocean liners, when time seemed to be more plentiful and travel a leisurely occupation!

The New Traction

On looking back as I write this, I have come to realise just how much I was enjoying my work during the closing years of Nine Elms mpd. I think the beginning of the final run down was the introduction of the 'Warship' diesels to work the Exeter services in 1964, following the transfer of the Salisbury-Exeter main line to the Western Region. The 'A.C.E.' ceased to run after the 1964 summer service. I was in No. 2 Link at the time and as the majority of the drivers in the top link were on the verge of retirement it was decided to train my link on the 'new traction'. Even so, there were drivers therein who were 14 years or so senior to me, such was the result of the former Southern Railway being over-staffed with locomotive crews following World War I and with the falling off of freight work. Very few footplate men had been recruited from 1921 until 1934. This was the year that I started engine cleaning and throughout my career I was just behind men who were much older than I. At New Cross Gate in 1934, the senior cleaners were married men with families and when they eventually became appointed firemen, after 20 years cleaning and spare firing, I was right behind them and was appointed as a fireman in just under six years. On the other hand, there were firemen who had been on the main line for 15 years or more, but were relatively better off than their slightly younger contemporaries in that they did have rostered work and regular pay rises within the grade. Therefore a few month's difference in seniority made its mark upon men in no uncertain way. It would have been a different story if the railway industry had been expanding instead of contracting following the 1923 forming of the four main line companies. On the Southern the extensive electrification made drivers, but not fast enough to absorb the vast number of firemen, and subsequently engine cleaners, who 'stood still' with the contraction of the steam engine side of the business.

Bibby Line – an Old Favourite

But, more about the 'Warships' and other prime movers in a later chapter and let us return to the halcyon days of the early sixties. One morning I booked on duty at 1.55am for 2.15am off the shed to work the 2.45am paper train to Bournemouth. My mate was Bob Payne and the engine allocated to us was MN No. 35020 *Bibby Line*, a grand engine. She had a modified tender, in which the coal space had been reduced so as to accommodate an extra 1,000 gallons of water, making a total of 6,000 gallons. The engine had been prepared and stood outside the R/F's office. As we walked to our charge, I thought 'there's not an over abundance of coal up there'. I climbed onto the footplate and checked the coal pile, it was neatly trimmed but only just visible, but I did not consider it necessary to return to the coal hopper to 'top up'. Anyway, the coalmen had gone to supper, as once the paper train engines had departed, there was a quiet period before incoming locos arrived off their duties. The next outgoing main line engine would have been for the Portsmouth line van train, about an hour after my own turn. So, up to Waterloo, Bob coupled on, and steam heat was put on to warm the three coaches on the front of the train. This was usually a platform full, to be worked out of No. 10 but with no assistance at the rear as the stock had been shunted out to release the loco which had worked it in around 11.15pm. Known at Waterloo as a 'shunt-release' movement, the train was returned to the same platform by a shunting engine after the train engine had gone to Nine Elms. It was usually a lengthy consumer of time to get a heavy train on the move from Waterloo without rear end assistance, but on this occasion, the superb *Bibby Line* made the job look easy. We galloped down past Loco Junction box with the safety valves blowing off, back ashpan damper wide open and Bob plying the shovel as though he intended to get enough coal into the firebox by Woking to get us to Bournemouth! But by some freak of chance, the tender was loaded with hard coal which burnt fiercely, and quickly. I called out to him, "Do you want to go into Bournemouth Loco for coal Bob?" "No, of course not", he answered. "Right then, ease that damper and control the boiler", I counselled. My mate did so, the steaming rate was reduced and we called at our booked stations, losing a van or two off the rear at Woking, Basingstoke, Eastleigh and finally Southampton, where all we had on was three coaches and two or three vans for Bournemouth. Now was the time to take stock of the coal position. I opened the door on the footplate which gave access to the tender coal space and peered in with the light from the fire – there was not a lot of coal there, certainly not more than two tons, but, it was Welsh coal and mostly small stuff at that. There were several things to be considered if coal was to be taken at Bournemouth Loco, firstly the signalman at the station would have to be advised that the paper train engine needed to go into Loco for coal. He in turn would advise the R/F who would make the necessary arrangements, ie, endeavour to clear the road to the coal crane and as the coalmen were on the verge of going home off the night shift, a Nine Elms' engine entering their domain at 5.45am was not received with open arms! On top of that, there was usually a tub of poor coal awaiting an unwanted visitor, possibly with a view to deterring future visits, unless it was absolutely necessary. There was also the time factor involved. If everything was running to time then it was a 5.40am arrival at the Central, the fireman would have to unhook from the train and place the tail lamp in position. The signalman set the road and pull off the required signal. Then we would have to make haste to Branksome, the next station down the line, and stop in the platform, the road to be set for the goods loop, which was traversed to Branksome Loco (ex-S&D), a pair of points pulled, the engine moved forward to the water column and the pipe put in etc. The time would now be about 6am and a Bournemouth fireman would appear to shovel the coal forward on the tender whilst the Nine Elms' crew did what was needed, ready to work up the 7.20am from Bournemouth West. The driver would look around his engine and feel the bearings, top up the cylinder gland oil cups, check the mechanical lubricators and so on. The fireman usually checked his fire, added coal in the back corners, filled up the boiler and washed down the footplate whilst the injector was on. As the area is a residential one, noise had to be kept to the minimum, and engines blowing off steam would soon have produced letters of complaint to the management. The driver would eventually get a note which began, "Please explain"! After these necessary chores it was breakfast time and the Branksome Loco shedman would have the water boiling in the kettle for the welcome 'cuppa' in the messroom.

On this particular morning, the Bournemouth fireman who was shovelling the coal forward completed the job in three minutes. His

Adams 0395 class 0-6-0 No. 30577 on the RCTS 'West Surrey' special from Waterloo to Victoria, via East Putney, Brookwood, Camberley, Ascot and Clapham Junction in November 1952. The safety valves blew hard at 145 psi and the vacuum brake leaked on at 120 psi, so a maximum margin of 25 psi meant careful attention to the boiler, and my fireman, Jim Sullivan, coped well.

(Peter Hay)

The RCTS 25th anniversary special on Sunday, 28th June 1953, was worked from Waterloo to Salisbury by D15 class 4-4-0 No. 30464. Driver Jerry Sartin kindly allowed me to work this train under the 'agreed substitute' rule prevalent in 1953. I am seen here, with Fireman Jim Hawkins, upon arrival at Salisbury, where the train was handed over to another crew with a T9.

Another ambitious RCTS special took a Brighton Atlantic from Waterloo to Guildford via Brentford and Chertsey, and was probably the only time a locomotive of this class worked the route. This was run on 6th February 1955 and my mate on this occasion was Fireman Bill Botten. No. 32421 *South Foreland* is seen here running in to Guildford.

Opposite, top: I went 'pass' to Stewarts Lane depot during Mr R. H. N. Hardy's time there, to work No. 34088 *213 Squadron* light engine to Fratton depot in readiness for the 'Royal' to Victoria via the Mid Sussex line the following day. In this official photograph I can be seen far left, with Fireman Evans, and with Mr Hardy, fourth from left.

Right: Fireman Les Hoath and I on the footplate of No. 30453 *King Arthur* on the 12.58pm Salisbury to Waterloo, 17th August 1960. Following the publication of *Nine Elms Engineman* in 1984 Les wrote to me saying, "You taught me more about engine-manship from both sides of the footplate than all the other so-called drivers put together!" Les left the service after several years at Wimbledon emu depot.

(Colin P. Walker)

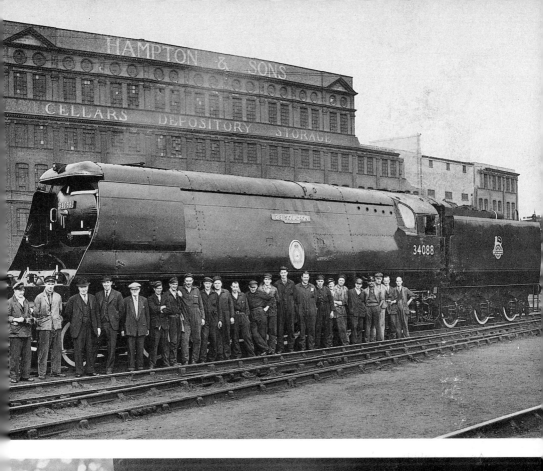

The view ahead from *King Arthur* later in the day on 17th August 1960, at Winchfield station.

(Colin P. Walker)

SNCF No. 231-K 83, seen en route to Vesoul. The mécanicien, a young man, *ran* round the engine, and underneath it, to feel every bearing. A pit appeared to be standard equipment at all main line stations in France where engines took water.

(George Barlow)

Two French mécaniciens at Bournemouth West on 3rd September 1962 with No. 34107 *Blandford Forum* behind. On my right is Andre Duteil and on the left is Henri Dutertre of Calais. Unfortunately I could not speak their language and they could not speak mine, so communication was by signs. Andre had a marvellous touch with the regulator and could start a 'West Country' without slipping, but would not touch the steam reverser!

(R. H. N. Hardy)

The record-breaking Gresley A4 Pacific, No. 60022 *Mallard* at Waterloo on Sunday, 23rd February 1963 when it worked an LCGB special to Exeter, returning via the former GWR route to Paddington. I was lucky enough to get the job, with my mate Bob Payne, for the first leg to Salisbury. We are seen at Waterloo awaiting departure.

(*George Barlow*)

Mallard was a superb loco, and I am seen here enjoying myself as we approached Wimbledon. This was not the fastest trip I had to Salisbury, but it seemed like it! I was sorry to have to step off this famous locomotive and it was a privilege to drive her. A. Earle Edwards was District Officer at Southampton, hence he was able to obtain a footplate pass.

(A. Earle Edwards)

"My loco" of Top Link firing days, as rebuilt. I considered No. 35020 *Bibby Line* to be the best of the class as rebuilt. Depicted at Salisbury – someone has burnt the smokebox door!

(G. Hounsell)

Left: I was given the job of working the 'Solway Ranger' rail tour, organised by the West Riding Branch of the RCTS on Saturday, 13th June 1964. This was after protracted negotiations at Nine Elms following the suggestion from Mr R. H. N. Hardy to the society organisers that they write to Mr Stanley Downes, the District Motive Power Officer, and ask for my services on the tour. A most interesting three days work it was and I am seen here at Leeds City station with Fireman Ken Seaby.

(Gavin Morrison)

Rebuilt 'Merchant Navy' No. 35012 *United States Lines* is far from home as it climbs towards Ais Gill Summit on one of the fastest recorded runs from the north, whilst working the RCTS 'Solway Ranger' special on 13th June 1964. I had told Ken that the only scenery he would see when we were going up hill would be floorboards and firehole! I kept him busier than on our own railway, but he stuck to his job like a good un. We did not see a motive power inspector during the whole time!

(John K. Morton)

The fireman's side view from No. 35026 *Lamport & Holt Line* whilst working an 'up' Bournemouth train approaching Roundwood Tunnel. The fireman was Alan Newman.

(*A. E. Hooker*)

No. 35023 *Holland-Afrika Line* on the occasion of the special high speed run of 15th October 1966, from Waterloo to Salisbury, with proceeds in aid of the Woking Homes. I gained the fastest ever recorded timing between milepost 51 (Worting Junction) and milepost 81 (Tunnel Junction) – 20 min 12 sec for the 30 miles – an average speed of 89.9 mph. The maximum was 101 mph at Andover, 62 over Grateley Summit and 99 at Porton. A good run. This picture shows the train between Winchfield and Hook, running at 80 mph.

(*Paul Riley*)

Holland-Afrika Line at Salisbury after its record breaking run from Waterloo on 15th October 1966. I had said to Arthur Jupp, our Inspector, "I am 'letting my hair down' today as this will be the last time I work a non stop to Salisbury". His reply was, "Alright Bert, I'll put a cloth over the speedometer!" My fireman was 'Rocker' Dedman, the first time we had worked together. Both outside big ends were very warm at Salisbury!

(B. C. Bending)

The driver's view from a Bulleid Pacific in original condition – approaching Otterbourne intermediate signals (Shawford 'up' road) on No. 34105 *Swanage*, which is now on the Mid-Hants Railway in fully restored condition. The view ahead is good on this occasion as the exhaust is drifting to the fireman's side.

(A. E. Hooker)

My last trip on a steam engine on a BR service train – the 08.10 boat train out of Waterloo on 26th June 1967. Photographed at Southampton, the engine is rebuilt 'Battle of Britain' No. 34060, formerly named *25 Squadron*. The fireman was M. Costello. This was a sad occasion and each trip before the final date of closure was an adventure – 'will she break down or will we get there?'

(Frank Bailey)

I am on the footplate of No. 34006 *Bude*, and she is in a sorry state on the scrap road. It is a long way from when we worked the Marylebone to Manchester in the 1948 Locomotive Exchanges.

Unhappily, now just a memory, the signal box at Loco Junction, as viewed from the cab of a Class 33 'Crompton'.

(A. R. W. Crowhurst)

The Waterloo to Exeter services were worked by 'Warship' diesel hydraulics after the section west of Salisbury was taken over by the Western Region. I am at the controls of a 'Warship' about 1965, before spectacles were needed.

Now bespectacled, I am driving an electric multiple unit during the six years I was at Slade Green – a 'convalescent home' after Waterloo Mixed Traction!

Driver Jerry Sartin and myself at Dungeness on the 15in gauge Romney, Hythe & Dymchurch Railway on a sunny summer afternoon.
(George Barlow)

I had never dreamt I would handle a broad gauge locomotive, and three years after retirement I was on the footplate of the replica *Iron Duke*, during its brief visit to Kensington Gardens, London at Easter 1985. The 'old firm' of Mr R. H. N. Hardy and A. E. H. exchange tales of the footplate. This loco needed careful handling to stop right – there was no brake on the locomotive, only a vacuum brake on the tender and this was silent, so I could not hear the air going into the brake system – somewhat disconcerting! However, a unique and wonderful occasion.

Overleaf: Bert Hooker in retirement, Easter 1985 – but still on the footplate – the *Iron Duke* broad gauge replica, whilst being demonstrated on a temporary track located, appropriately between the Albert Hall and the Albert Memorial. . .

(John Click)

comments were drastic and to the point, "You ain't got enough coal driver", he announced. I answered, "Yes we have", and with a shrug of disbelief he departed to the messroom where Bob was making the tea. There is invariably coal laying around a loco depot and Branksome was no exception so, for a few moments I busied myself tossing up the lumps of the now precious fuel on to the tender of No. 35020. I estimated two to three hundredweight was gleaned from the ground around our engine and events subsequently proved that that time was well spent! I climbed into *Bibby Line*'s cab for a last check around and to wash my hands. I opened the tender door to appraise the coal situation; none fell onto the footplate and the door opened smoothly over the top of the 'black diamonds'. I thought of the time that Bill Woods and his fireman, named Jackman, worked the up 'Belle' on 28 cwt of coal with MN No. 35014 *Nederland Line* when she was fitted with the coal weighing tender that was 'floating around' at odd times. Bill was an exceptionally light engineman and I though that what he could do then I was going to do my best to emulate him now, indeed it was a case of having to as coming off the train to obtain coal would cause a serious delay. Before leaving the footplate I glanced again into the firebox. Bob had followed my advice and kept a good 'poultice' down the sides and back corners and with the ashpan damper virtually closed the boiler was well under control. I was mentally planning the trip ahead and weighing up the possibility of having to take on a pilot at some point, bearing in mind where an engine was likely to be obtained with the minimum of delay, and if so, how to word the "Please explain" note that would inevitably follow!

After partaking of our sandwiches and tea, the tea can was rinsed out and filled with water in case a drink was needed on the trip to London. We climbed aboard *Bibby Line*, I created a brake and applied it so that my mate could take off the tender handbrake, a touch on the whistle to let the signalman know that we were ready to depart for the West. The depot exit signal cleared, and with steam issuing from the cylinder drain cocks, No. 35020 heaved herself into motion. Once out of the depot the line fell quite steeply to the station and the ear-splitting noise from the drain cocks ceased because the regulator was closed as soon as the engine was rolling downhill. The coupling up completed, but there was no steam heat, thank goodness, and the vacuum brake created, I got down to check that the brake cylinder pistons on the coaches were down and the blocks free on the wheels as I did not require a 'sticking' or rubbing coach brake to hinder progress. If a brake piston had not released fully then it was a simple expedient to 'pull the strings' and partially destroy the vacuum to allow the brake piston to fall to the bottom of the cylinder. All being well in that department, I rejoined Bob on the footplate where he had opened the ashpan damper and fettled up his fire with the pricker. I reminded him of our dire coal situation. "Golden rules now Bob. No blowing off, half to two thirds of a glass of water only, high superheat and you must make every shovel of coal 'tell' – little and often and *never*, unless it is necessary, use the fireirons. If you're not a fireman now you will be at the end of this trip!" He just grinned and acceded to my instructions.

For my part there definitely had to be no slipping, extra gentle starts – no rapid acceleration to burn the coal at a more rapid rate and above all, no running before time at junctions which may lead to being stopped and making unnecessary inroads upon our coal. As *Bibby Line* had a 6,000 gallon tender we did not take water at Southampton so as to be ready to move immediately the guard waved 'right away'. In any case, the three minute allowance at the station had been whittled away somewhat due to my extra gentle starts from all the stations between Bournemouth and Brokenhurst. From there we ran to Southampton, called at Winchester and then fast to Waterloo. Bob was doing well, maintaining around 240psi, water nicely in sight in the gauge glass and giving me hot steam which was used to the best advantage. I never used full regulator and a short cut-off, regardless of what was going on around me! Most Southern engines protest at that method of driving in various ways, usually by means of a fearful noise up the chimney or a terrific clatter from the driving axleboxes, so I invariably ran the engine between 20 and 30 per cent cut-off adjusted the regulator to produce a smoothly running engine and a contented fireman.

The station master at Winchester usually saw this train away as it was an important one, carrying a host of 'City Top Brass' to their offices in London, so a 10am arrival at Waterloo was very desirable. The secret of running the train was to ensure that you approached Woking Junction at the booked time, 9.34am – it was easy to arrive there at 9.32am, only to get stopped as a Guildford 'slow' was booked across the junction in front of the 7.20am, and if that happened then a late arrival at the terminus was inevitable. I had a note written out to give to the station master – "Please ask Control to ensure that I am not stopped en route to London otherwise we shall be out of coal". But he wasn't there! *Bibby Line* was not pressed too hard up the bank from Winchester, it was 'gently does it', but even so, the great locomotive made the job look easy, gradually accelerating under the urge of superheated steam. Worting Junction was passed under clear signals nearly a minute late and on the slightly falling gradients beyond Basingstoke, the MN needed to be restricted somewhat otherwise she would have made up several minutes to Woking Junction. That I did not wish for, so it was a case of 'hang back' conserve what little coal remained on the tender and let the old girl float along on a breath of steam. Brookwood was passed at 9.31^{1}/$_{2}$am – 2^{1}/$_{2}$ minutes to run the three miles to Woking Junction, but on the falling gradient of 1 in 314 our speed was increasing smoothly. That Guildford electric was surely over the junction by now. It was, as indicated by the welcome green light near milepost 26, and *Bibby Line* swept through Woking at 80mph and the job was as good as done. There was just over 25 minutes to run the remaining 25 miles to Waterloo. Curiously enough the 7.20am did not have a passing time for Hampton Court Junction shown in the WTT but it was a case of 'best foot forward' to that point, so as to be able to observe the 70 mph from Surbiton to New Malden. Thereafter it was 60 mph to Clapham Junction which was passed dead on 9.53am and so we slid into Waterloo at 10 o'clock – one shovelful of coal left! I asked Bob, "Why didn't you put that on?", and he quipped, "Had to save some for our relief, and in any case it stopped the shovel rattling!" I must say that I signed off duty at Vauxhall somewhat relieved that the train had been run satisfactorily, with no other train delay beyond my control to hinder progress. I also enjoyed a feeling of contentment that my judgement of the job was not at fault, although I doubt if it would have been attempted on any other loco. In my humble opinion, *Bibby Line* was the best rebuilt MN but doubtless other drivers would disagree.

A 'Battle of Britain' V a Mogul

This economical running was in direct contrast to what took place on an alternative date. Bob and I were working the 11.12am from Bournemouth to Waterloo with BoB No. 34057 *Biggin Hill*. The load was the normal eleven coaches, about 380 tons. Progress had been satisfactory to Basingstoke despite the failure of the steam reverser to remain where I wanted the cut-off, 25 to 30 per cent. On leaving the station I looked back to see the connecting stopping service to Waterloo just leaving at 1.13pm, the engine was a U class 2-6-0 tender engine hauling three coaches and I judged the Guildford men aboard her intended to catch us up before their first station stop at Hook. I communicated my thoughts to my mate who cried, "Don't let them pass us Bert!" "Alright", I answered, "But you'll have to shovel some coal." As I opened the regulator wide, No. 34057 developed a song of power and rapidly accelerated, and Bob was busy with the 'blade'. I looked back again and the 'U-boat' was steadily gaining and a blue haze was coming from his chimney, indicating good superheat. It is nearly six miles from Basingstoke to Hook and as we went by the distant signals for Hook our speedometer indicated just over 80 mph! The Guildford crew kept their charge at it until our footplates were level, both grinning at us on the 'Battle of Britain', the driver then had to shut off and brake for Hook. I saw him a week or so later and asked, "Did you stop alright at Hook on the day you passed me?" He assured me that he did, but to this day, I have my doubts as he had but a light train, barely 100 tons and the steam brake on the engine would be cold, and his braking distance would certainly have been less than a mile! It is surprising how great is the distance required to halt a light weight train from 80+mph.

Steam Loco Lubrication

On the subject of steam brakes, the lubrication of these was required to be done by the driver preparing the engine before going off the shed and it was a chore which was missed as often as it was done. On the Bulleid

Pacifics a ⁵⁄₈in open spanner was required to remove the plug on the steam pipe leading to the brake cylinders, about an eggcup full of thick oil was poured into the plughole and the plug replaced. Following this, re-opening the main steam cock to the vacuum ejector the oil was then blown into the brake cylinders for lubrication purposes to avoid a sticking or seized brake on the locomotive whilst out on the road. The spanner was apt to slip off the plug during its removal and to this day I carry a scar on my left forearm where the skin was burnt off when my arm went onto the hot pipe. Needless to say, I uttered a few well chosen words to alleviate the sudden pain!

On the BR Standards a neat arrangement of taps on a pair of brass oil receptacles were screwed into a steel base at the foot of the vacuum brake pillar. The idea was to knock the tap gently with a spanner to loosen it, then remove it by hand, then fill the receptacle with thin oil, which would be used on a displacement basis. Fine – until someone overtightened the tap, in which case, the whole was screwed out of the base, so a drop of thick oil was given direct into the hole and the oil receptacle replaced, following which the vacuum main steam cock was re-opened. It was dangerous to attempt to introduce oil into the system with the latter in the open position, a spout of near boiling oil in one's face is, to say the least, somewhat distasteful!

One afternoon, I booked on at 4.59pm at Vauxhall station as a passenger to Waterloo, to work the 5.39pm commuter train to Salisbury, stopping at all stations after Woking, so an efficient brake on the engine and tender was essential. The engine, a BR Class 5, had just backed onto the train and was coupled on, my mate and I climbed aboard, and after the usual pleasantries were exchanged, I asked the driver, "Did you oil the steam brake?" He answered in the negative and as there was nearly 20 minutes to starting time, I decided to do the chore myself. The train brake was destroyed and the chamber side on the loco was released, after the small jet was closed. The necessary spanner was obtained from the toolbox and I set to work. The tap was too stubborn to move so I put the spanner onto the squared section of the oil receptacle, it moved all right, too easily in fact, as the soft brass thread broke completely away exposing a ¼in hole which would emit scalding steam every time the brake was applied. We were potentially a failure and I would not be very popular if I requested another engine so near to starting time. I looked around on the ground in the Dock for a suitable spigot of wood, found one, and took it onto the footplate. Now for some whittling practice until one shaved end fitted into the hole. I poured thick oil therein, as, after all, that was the object of the exercise. The spigot was rammed into the aperture and clumped home with the hand hammer, a couple of dirty cloths were laid across the repair which were kept in position with the coal pick. I gingerly applied the steam brake; not enough leaking steam to worry about, then re-created the train brake and we were ready to go. A wary eye was kept on my temporary repair job and I was thankful to get into Salisbury Loco without incident. The leading fitter was approached and I spilled out the sorry story. "Not to worry," he said, "I'll get a new one fitted". "The base of the old one will have to be drilled out" I replied, thinking that was likely to be an awkward job. "No problem," the worthy character went on, "It will be done before you go off the shed for your return trip. You go and get your supper". I thanked him and my mate and I went into the enginemens' lobby to make a can of tea and eat sandwiches. The Standard Class 5 was standing outside the shed, the offending steam brake plug had been replaced and was steam tight. On the trip back to Nine Elms Goods, I resolved that the oiling of the steam brake was not to be attempted with only 15 minutes to go before starting time.

An Inter-Regional Troop Train

On Saturday 16th February, my mate, Bob Payne and I, were booked on duty at 3.20pm to go passenger to Fratton mpd to prepare an engine and work an empty troop train from the adjacent carriage sidings to Willesden. The ultimate destination was somewhere north of the border. We reported to the Running Shift Foreman, who indicated that we had a low number Standard Class 5, which had worked the loaded train in some time during the day. The R/F said, "I'll send a driver out to assist you driver." "I don't require assistance," I replied, but he went on to say, "It will give him something to do as he is without a mate." I shrugged my shoulders and within a few moments a young driver appeared. "I'll oil around if you like," he announced. I gave him the oil feeder and said, "O.K., carry on then, I'll do the steam brake and have a clean up on the footplate". We both set about our respective tasks and Bob began his side of the preparation business, trimming and lighting the oil lamps, checking the sand boxes, fire and ashpan, etc. After a few moments, my assistant came back to the footplate to tell me that he was going to see the fitter as the left side small end cotter was well down. I got down to appraise the job – the cotter *was* well down, but judging by the amount of dirt and oil on the lower end it had been down for sometime! The fitter duly arrived and said very quietly to me, "I had noticed it driver, but now my attention has been drawn to it, I've got to 'stop' her." I answered him, "She got down here alright and she'll go back to where she belongs if I had my way." "I'm sorry about this, but I'm afraid you'll have to ask for another engine", the fitter went on. So, there was nothing for it but to go and see the R/F and spill out the story of the left small end cotter. He wasn't exactly overjoyed at the disclosure and announced, "The only engine I've got is 31806." (This was formerly *River Torridge* of the ill-fated 'River' class tanks which were rebuilt to tender locomotives at Brighton in 1928. After conversion the names were not perpetuated.)

At this news, I did not become elated, guessing that the condition of the 2-6-0 was not pristine. Whilst I was not too impressed with the Standard 5s for cold weather work, at least the one we had been allocated originally would have been superior to the erstwhile 'River' tank. So No. 31806 was prepared, my assistant oiling around the 'peg work' whilst I got on with filling the hydrostatic lubricator, the piston valve guides, and not overlooking the steam brake, all with the quota of superheat oil. My mate Bob thought it all a big joke and I refrained from mentioning that a 2-6-0 would descend Haslemere Bank with considerable more liveliness than a 4-6-0. He would learn in due course! Our train was reached in short time in the carriage sidings, Bob coupled on, steam heat turned on and a brake created. The load was seven, six-wheeled bogie sleeping cars, altogether a fair load for a nondescript 2-6-0. The guard tried the brake, I re-created it, the siding signal cleared, a hand signal from the Yard Foreman and we were on our way. Progress was normal along the fairly level track to Havant, round the corner and the regulator was put right over for the climb up Buriton Bank. Bob had got her warmed up and No. 31806 was steaming well and climbed steadily up the bank to the summit. Approaching Buriton Tunnel I cracked the blower, closed the regulator then immediately reopened it on to about half the first port as the gradient was now in our favour down towards Petersfield. The 'distant' was off and 31806 was beginning to run hard, probably doing 60 mph, at least it felt like it, as conditions on the footplate had become somewhat lively.

Bob's fire had begun to creep forward down the sloping grate so he needed to place a few shovelfuls 'in the door', as it was necessary to keep the back end of the firebox well up ready for more hard pulling up the 1 in 80 gradient ahead from Liss towards Liphook. After about two miles, the gradient eased but was still mostly against the engine, with the final two miles up to Haslemere steepened to 1 in 100. I think my mate had the same feeling as myself. I would sooner be going uphill than downhill on our 2-6-0! Once through Haslemere the gradient changed and soon we were galloping downhill on 1 in 80. Speed rose rapidly under the merest breath of steam, the engine 'hunting' in a disconcerting manner. I applied the steam brake slightly to steady the old girl as I did not desire the 70 mph speed ceiling to be breached. The three miles of 1 in 80 down was covered in under three minutes although it seemed considerably longer. Whitley distant signal was showing green, heralding the approach to a short sharp rise up for a mile through the station, a not unwelcome respite in the mad gyrations of No. 31806 as the change of gradient did have a calming effect upon our charge, but not for long, as the gradient changed and we were charging down towards Milford, nearly two miles away. The one time *River Torridge* soon resumed her thrashing about but after that station was passed the gradient eased considerably and approaching Godalming I had to apply the train brake in order to observe the 50mph permanent speed restriction through to Farncombe. Footplate noise had subsided, and what a relief it was to be riding reasonably smoothly. I called to Bob, "The excitement's over. How about doing it all again tomorrow?" His reply was partially unprintable, but I got the message!

We rolled to a stop at Guildford station in what seemed an almost uncanny silence. "Put the pipe in Bob, the signalman isn't ready yet and we may get messed around up at Willesden", I remarked. He concurred and whilst water was gushing into the tender I made a quick check of the engine bearings – everything was fine, no corks thrown, just warm big ends, etc. The remainder of the trip was made at a more sedate pace, up through Woking, then off the main line at Byfleet Junction to go via Chertsey and Richmond to Clapham Junction, thence on to the West London Extension to Mitre Bridge (Willesden), where Bob uncoupled and we went forward into a siding to reverse and await a pathway to return light to Nine Elms mpd.

With the modernisation to colour light signals under the control of one power signal box, the Willesden complex did not hold the terror it had previously done for us Nine Elms men. Stewarts Lane, Hither Green and Feltham men had regular freight duties there and were more familiar with the area, especially if they had had firing experience also. If one was not too sure of any particular move then a word to the signalman in the box from one of the numerous 'phones around, would soon bring reassurance. Those chaps were very helpful once you indicated you were a Southern man and needed a little guidance.

To go back to the Pompey main line, there is no doubt that the '4 corridor multiple unit sets', made up to twelve coaches were heavy on the track, causing more maintenance thereon with their nose hung motors and more unsprung weight than the previously used main line steam engines, including the 'King Arthurs', 'Lord Nelsons', 'Schools' and 'Remembrance' class 4-6-0s. As far as I am aware, the Nine Elms four-cylinder 'Nelsons' only gravitated to the Portsmouth line during the winter when there was less Bournemouth and Salisbury daytime work to be undertaken and a Pompey job was put in the Top Link on a temporary basis for a few weeks. This leads me to stress the fact that once a main line steam train had gone past Woking Junction the riding qualities of the engine improved quite noticeably, whilst the reverse was the case when approaching Woking from the westerly direction, the facing points encountered from there to London invariably caused the loco to dip and sway when running hard, but the multiple unit trains seemed unaffected. So, old 31806 was running hard over tracks that had taken a beating over the years from the electric "Nelsons", colloquially known thus because they had only one look-out window, the corridor section occupying a vast area of the unit front, and its lateral movement was startling until one became used to it. The other small section of the front was used by the headcode number – all quite primitive compared with modern stock.

A Hot Box on a Boat Train

How the driver became attuned to the locomotive he was driving is illustrated by the following: On 17th August 1964, my mate, John Williams and I, were on an evening boat train to Southampton Old Docks, our loco was BoB No. 34090, *Sir Eustace Missenden*, a good strong engine but reputedly one that did not make your head ache with blowing off steam, but John was a good fireman and was having little difficulty keeping her round. In short, we were having a good trip. Approaching Farnborough I felt the engine pause in her stride, a few seconds later I caught a whiff that can only come from a hot axlebox. "We've got trouble John", I called out. "What's that, what is it?", he answered, glancing at his pressure gauge, which was showing about 230 psi and the boiler water gauge indicating two-thirds of a glass. "We've got a hot box, can't you smell it?" I questioned him. John sniffed the air, "Now I can, what are you going to do Bert?" "We'll have another engine at Basing so run your fire down", I replied. So now to get the message to the Running Shift Foreman at Basingstoke mpd that I required another engine. I checked the road ahead, and automatic signals just a mile apart were all 'off'. I searched my pocket for an old stencil notice and wrote a short message – "Signalman, please advise Basing that I require another engine, 34090 – hot box. A. Hooker, Driver." A piece of worsted wool was obtained from the cupboard, the message was wrapped around a piece of coal and tied with the wool, I had eased the regulator and 34090 was slowing down. Approaching Fleet I blew a series of short whistles which brought the signalman to his window, a wave of my arm and then I pitched the message on to the platform near to the box. The signalman waved, acknowledging that he understood the charade. I hoped he would be able to read my script as there was no telling if it had sustained damage during its 50 mph dive onto the station.

I did not press *Sir Eustace Missenden* unduly as it was prudent to keep the speed down, as if the axlebox overheated badly there was always the possibility of it seizing in the horncheeks, which could possibly lead to a derailment. As I had no real knowledge of the condition of the axlebox it was better to toddle along quietly to Basingstoke where I hoped, there would be a fresh engine. I stopped on the station ramp, and the Basingstoke R/F was waiting. I reached the ground in a hurry to see smoke rising up from the middle right side axlebox, it was hot all right. A few more miles and it would have been on fire! The R/F was George Webster, whom I knew in my New Cross Gate days, when he fired to 'Cocky' Verral on the Top Link there. "Hello Bert, I haven't a man in the place", he greeted me, "You'll have to take this one in and bring out 73016. I've pushed the fire over." John had uncoupled our 'Battle of Britain' from the train and had appraised the guard of the situation as he had come to the front to ascertain the cause of the out of course stop. George went on, "The signalman knows the drill, away you go". The platform starting signal was 'off', I set 34090 into protesting motion up over the points, then back into the loco area where George pulled the points for the road he wanted her in. John had run the fire down nicely and had filled the boiler, the engine was secured, reverser in mid-gear, cylinder drains opened and tender handbrake on, vacuum brake small jet closed. Gathering our personal gear we boarded BR Class 5 No. 73016, the fire was burning up well, and George Webster had acted outside his province as a Supervisor in pushing the fire over the grate – he merely did it to expedite the job in the absence of his footplate staff, to minimize unavoidable delay. John made a quick check of the tools on the engine, the tank was full and the coal stacked safely. For my part I checked that all the corks were in situ on the side rods, etc. and that there was oil in the piston gland cups and in the mechanical lubricators. John tried the injectors, they were fine, I tried the vacuum brake, no problems and as we moved forward George telephoned the signalman that we were ready to rejoin the train. As we dropped back to the depot exit, I mentally congratulated the unknown crew who had left No. 73016 in a 'ready for the road condition'. It was not long ere we were coupled onto our train again, the brake created and tested and we were then on the way to the Old Docks, with a delay at Basingstoke of just under half an hour. It was unwise to thrash the train into motion when leaving Basingstoke as the fire was not in the condition to support that, so matters were taken sensibly until we had passed Wootten box. John had the fire going nicely by then and No. 73016 had warmed up and once through Roundwood Tunnel on the falling gradient of 1 in 250 for eleven miles, the BR Standard really flew. It was obvious that a punctual arrival in the Docks was out of the question but I do not think the ocean liner sustained a late start. I hope note, and if it did, I did not get a note headed "Please explain etc."! Although I guess it was not beyond the bounds of possibility that Waterloo Headquarters may have had to answer a *billet-doux* from the shipping company re the late arrival of the boat train in Southampton Docks. If they did, then reference would have been made to the Control log of the day in question.

A Royal Train to Andover

The only time as a driver, I had Royalty travelling on my train was on Monday, 4th November 1963. Notification was given to me several days prior that the Princess Royal would be travelling on the 9am from Waterloo to Andover. It was not my rostered turn of duty, so the news was somewhat of a surprise. Apparently, the job needed to be covered and as I was the nearest spare man it fell to me. I looked at the roster to ascertain which fireman should be there, and it was J. J. Smith, a chap who, unhappily was not too particular about his appearance whilst he was at work. However, that did not detract from his work capabilities, and he was a willing worker. So I approached him at the first opportunity to 'put him in the picture' re the special person on the train. I showed him the note from Mr Gilchrist, our Shedmaster, and put the question to him, "Any chance of putting on a collar and tie, along with some clean overalls and boots next Monday John?" To my relief he did not take umbrage and assured me he would not let me down. When we booked on at Vauxhall station at 8.20pm on the 4th, I was pleasantly surprised.

John looked almost resplendent, his boots shone, new overalls on, a white shirt with a good necktie, face clean and shaven and to crown it all, a new cap! He must have had the new gear stored against such an occasion. So, we went up to Waterloo to the front of our train, just in time to see a clean MN coming over Westminster Bridge. All the available cleaners at the depot must have been put to work on No. 35017 *Belgian Marine* as she looked quite presentable.

Eddie Dye, (who was my fireman on the day Lester Piggot won the Derby on 'Never say Die') had prepared the engine with Inspector Danny Knight in attendance and, as is usual under the circumstances, would ride on the engine as far as Salisbury. Eddie's fireman coupled on, under the watchful eye of the Inspector. When they returned to the footplate I opened the vacuum brake small jet and watched the train pipe needle slowly rise to the regulation 21 inches. The carriage warming cock was opened progressively until a steady 50psi was showing on the gauge. Next, the guard made the regulation brake test after which I quickly restored the 21 inches of vacuum in the brake system and then went down to ascertain if the brake pistons were down on the first two coaches. I was prepared to go the whole length of the train if necessary to 'pull the strings' if the pistons were not down. However, they were, as they should be, provided the incoming driver of the empty stock had not inadvertently created more than 21in of vacuum. Satisfied, I returned to the footplate to partake of the inevitable cup of tea. Eddie and his mate had done their stuff and *Belgian Marine* was ready for the road. Promptly, at 9am the 'right away' was given and I set the MN into steady motion with no slipping of the driving wheels as it invariably causes snatches in the train and I did not wish to make a bad impression on our passengers, particularly the Royal one! Engine No. 35017 was in good order and made the job a 'snip', responding well to my administrations of the regulator and cut-off. There was a temporary speed restriction over a renewed road bridge at New Malden, 'dead slow' were the instructions and which were duly observed, costing about four minutes of running time.

We called at Surbiton and Woking, still 'four down'. I did not press *Belgian Marine* unduly to Basingstoke and regained only a minute. The allowance from there to Andover was 21 minutes, quite a sharp timing and Danny asked me, "Will we be right time at Andover Bert?" I answered in the affirmative. John had worked a good fire into the old girl's firebox so he was ready when I opened out the engine once the train was on the move. Acceleration up to Worting Junction was good and once beyond the half-way point between Oakley and Overton, the gradient changed and the Pacific began to get a move on. I was careful that the 85 mph ceiling in force at the time was not breached on the falling grades through Whitchurch and Hurstbourne, and after the latter station there was a mile uphill of 1 in 275, a pull on the regulator ensured there was not a falling off of speed. Once over that small summit the regulator was eased, John was looking out for the outer distant for Andover, he raised his arm as soon as he saw it in the 'off' position, and as it came into view from my side of the footplate I shut off steam and began to apply the brake. A nice gentle stop was made at Andover with the big station clock on the 'down' platform indicating 10.23am, right time arrival.

Danny was pleased, and so was I, as I thought that I should have hustled the MN a little more between Woking and Basingstoke, but all was well and proved once again that a 'Merchant Navy' was a most capable locomotive. A brass band on the platform was making musical noises to greet the Princess Royal, watched with interest by the three of us. I asked Danny if he would like to drive the engine to Salisbury, but to my surprise he declined and I never knew why! Usually, a former loco man jumps at the opportunity to have the regulator when it is offered. I knew one inspector who felt that driving the engine was somewhat beneath him, but Danny Knight did not impress me as leaning towards snobbery of that description. After all, a loco inspector in the steam era came up through the ranks and though they had vast firing experience their driving experience was limited, at least on main line work.

Danny did not last too long in the new traction era, having reached retirement age, and I am sorry to say that he had a most unhappy 'Senior Citizen' period. He was standing, with his wife on the pavement at Clapham Junction, apparently waiting for a bus, when a motor vehicle mounted the pavement and crushed Mrs Knight against the wall, causing her death and injuring Danny. After this, the grapevine story indicated that he went to live with his brother in the Eastleigh area, subsequently becoming ill with shingles and did not survive its onslaught. Danny only rode with me on that one occasion as a driver, but during my firing he rode quite frequently, especially when he was responsible for the selection of the 1948 Interchange crews. A knowledgable and popular man who did not deserve his untimely demise. When the occasion demanded, he could, and would, dress down a footplate crew who transgressed, i.e. excessive smoke and blowing off steam, or giving a footplate ride to unauthorised people. (I came within the last category!)

3

R. H. N. Hardy

ONE MORNING DURING the winter of 1952/3, I, as Chairman of the Nine Elms Mutual Improvement Class in company with the Secretary, Tim Crowley, was invited to a conference at Stewarts Lane depot, together with other depot MIC representatives. This was to discuss the desirability of engendering more interest in the movement. The host MIC was, very naturally present, and the meeting was presided over by Mr R. H. N. Hardy, the Stewarts Lane Shedmaster, recently appointed to the position from Ipswich mpd Eastern Region. The findings of the meeting are now lost to me except for one request I made of the chairman at the close of the meeting. A pile of photographs reposed upon his desk (the meeting having taken place in Mr Hardy's office). "May I look at the photos Sir," I asked. "Of course you may," he replied, "You came over from Nine Elms didn't you? Are you interested in the photographs?" "I'll say I am", I answered, and on looking through them they were mainly of the Eastern Region, but no matter, for they were photographs of steam engines and the men who worked and cared for them. I quickly warmed to the 'Guvnor' as he became known, through a mutual love of the steam engine. The conversation became easy – "What link are you in Bert, when did you start on the job and how long have you been at Nine Elms?" I gave a brief résumé of my career to date." I began cleaning at New Cross Gate in 1934, appointed fireman at Nine Elms – 1st April, 1940, fired on the Bulleid Pacific's during the 1948 Loco Exchanges, appointed Driver – 1st April 1949, and am currently in No. 6 Link."

"How far down the line do you go in that gang, what roads do you sign for? Our young drivers at Stewarts Lane go anywhere and are encouraged to do so." "I sign for everywhere, except the 'Old Docks', but it is an event to get booked on a main line job as we have so many spare men in the 'Pilot Gang' (Main Line spare Link) and some of them look down their noses if ambitious young drivers like myself are 'collared' for a Bournemouth or Salisbury job, ie. someone fails to show up for a turn, but I do change over for a Basingstoke job occasionally, usually the 7.54pm 'down' in the evening and back with the Sidmouth Milk. A driver friend of mine in No. 3 Link is failing in health and if I am rostered on

Nine Elms Goods or Clapham Yard shunting or an afternoon tank gang job, we make the changeover as I don't mind a later turn provided it is a 'runner'." Mr Hardy went on – "Would you mind if I came with you one evening when next you get that job? I'll get a footplate pass so you won't have to worry on that score." I must confess that I was taken somewhat by surprise with this request, but I quickly answered in the affirmative, as it was, to say the least, rather unusual for a Shedmaster to ride engines for the sheer love of it, especially during the evening! Little did I know then how my horizons were to be broadened by a simple request to peruse a pile of photographs.

On Monday 14th September 1953, I had acquired the 7.54pm Waterloo to Basingstoke, booking on duty at 7.11pm. I had notified Mr Hardy a few days beforehand, confirming my change-over of turns, following the provisional arrangements made with Jim Dawson a couple of weeks earlier, and which served Mr Hardy a date to keep clear if possible. I had the same job the following evening so there was a choice for him. I dare not make the change-over official until nearer the date of 14th/15th September, as there was always the possibility that Jim would go on the sicklist at short notice, due to him suffering with bronchial disorders. If that proved to be the case then 'change-overs' would not be honoured by the roster clerk and the arrangements would have to be cancelled. Anyway, Mr Hardy walked along Wandsworth Road from Stewarts Lane and we met at the top of Brooklands Road at 7pm, proceeding thence to the entrance of the great LSWR premier depot.

I signed on duty, collected what late notices were to hand and walked up to the shed. Our engine, a Urie N15 'King Arthur', No. 30751 *Etarre*, was standing at the water column on the corner of the shed, the preparing crew carrying out the finishing touches before handing over the engine. We went on into the shed, I to check the late notice case and peruse the daily alteration sheet whilst my friend cast his eye upon the rows of engines standing there, doubtless thinking that he could find work for them over at Stewarts Lane. As locomotive withdrawals had not seriously commenced on the modern classes there was a good variety present. Even more a few years previously, when the Drummond T14s, K10s and L11s were to be seen. During the earlier part of 1953 we had V2s from King's Cross and "Black 5s" from the LM Region, plus the odd 'Britannia' on loan following the temporary withdrawal of the 30 'Merchant Navy' Pacifics for sonic axle testing after No. 35020 *Bibby Line* came to grief on 24th April near Crewkerne with a fractured driving axle. When I was firing on that engine regularly on the Top Link in 1947, I never dreamt that the 'old girl' would be the subject of so much drama six years later! But, by the end of May or early June, all the on-loan engines had departed whence they came and Nine Elms resumed the ordinary lifestyle of the day.

To get back to the story, I found my fireman, a lad named Armitage and introduced him to Mr Hardy, omitting to mention who he was and merely indicating he was a friend of mine from the Eastern Section. We boarded *Etarre*, which was well prepared, exchanged a few words with the crew, created a brake, checked there was not another engine moving in the vicinity, and I opened the regulator gently and the N15 crept towards the depot exit signal. I 'blew up' for that signal, it cleared as we approached it, and I was thankful for that, as a standing start there on the steep gradient was invariably a potential problem with a boiler full of water and cold cylinders. We then passed the next elevated ground signal, and ran along to the bracket post which would give us access to the 'up' lines into Waterloo. After a 'down' train had gone by, then an 'up', the Loco Junction signalman (who could have been Vic Davis, whose son is now a driver at Norwood, after firing at Nine Elms) pulled off the left-hand signal which meant 'up the main' and soon we were on our way to Waterloo, a ritual which had been performed countless times over the years. Soon the N15 had buffered up to our train, which was well down the platform, indicating a short one, five or six bogie coaches and a van or two. With the coupling up completed, the steam heat on and the brake ready for the guard to test it, it was now the time to partake of a cup of tea and a chat with Mr Hardy re our Urie. He was familiar with the Maunsell N15s but our charge was one of the forerunners of the class and was not quite so modern, with short travel piston valves, a 180psi boiler, a high-domed cab and a live steam injector on the driver's side, and an exhaust injector on the fireman's side. The 'King Arthurs' all looked roughly the same to the general public, but to railwaymen and the enthusiast there was a deal of difference though in detail.

At 7.54pm we received the 'right away', my mate had fettled up the fire and on full first regulator *Etarre* marched the train away from Waterloo. As soon as the wheels had revolved two or three times I began to notch up, so before the platform starter was passed, she was in 50 per cent cut-off, and once over Westminster Bridge the cut-off was reduced to 40 per cent and as speed increased the cut-off was reduced one notch at a time, equivalent to $2\frac{1}{2}$ per cent. By the time we had passed Vauxhall cut-off was 30 per cent and No. 30751 was going well, the boiler had responded to Armitage's work, the exhaust injector was singing its song and the pressure gauge was close to 180psi. As we went by the carriage washer in West London Sidings I closed the regulator to let the engine gradually lose speed so as to obey the 40 mph permanent speed restriction through the Junction. No speedometers on the engines in 1953, it all revolved around the driver's judgement of speed, and a quietly running engine in 'good nick' was often deceiving to the crew, and many a speed restriction has been taken liberally, often in excess of the 10 per cent margin supposedly allowed by the P W engineer. But, on this occasion, *Etarre* rode through the curves at Clapham Junction easily, and approaching the colour light signal at the country end of the platform I re-opened the regulator on to full first valve, advanced the cut-off one notch to $32\frac{1}{2}$ per cent then cracked the big valve on the regulator in order to lift our train up through Clapham Cutting. My mate had turned off the injector as I put steam on again because the water was near to the top of the glass, plus the fact that to leave an injector on after a 'shut off' was a sure way to knock a boiler cold. Going through Earlsfield the regulator was opened wide, then closed and immediately put back on to the first full port and the cut-off adjusted to 30 per cent again.

The N15 was going well enough under these relatively easy conditions to time the train, and it was only on rising gradients that the 'big valve' was opened to keep speed around the 60/65 mph mark, such as up through Walton to Weybridge. The 31-minute allowance to Woking was completed nicely, watched with some interest by our guest. "Almost a billiard table railway", he commented, "A bit different working out of Victoria." I agreed, and to my surprise, Mr Hardy went on, "May I do the firing to Basingstoke"? I looked at my mate, who nodded in the affirmative, "Help yourself, I'll give you ample notice when I'll shut off", I answered. I think young Armitage was thinking along the same lines as myself! 'This may prove interesting, I wonder how far we'll get before we'll be down the nick!' But I was due for a second surprise. The 'Guv', turned off the injector as we had $^3/_4$ of a glass, then picked up the shovel, turned it over and peered at the fire, a little prod with it close up under the door, and as the shovel was withdrawn, he put up the half door with the blade, after which it was returned to the coal pile. The guard was showing a green light. "Right away" I called, opening the regulator and *Etarre* moved smoothly away, no point in hurrying as there was a 15 mph permanent restriction on the local line across Woking Junction. Once clear of that I put the regulator into the 'big valve' and adjusted the cut-off to the favourite 30 per cent. Mr Hardy now commenced firing. As soon as two or three shovelfuls had gone into the firebox I knew he had done it before, he was no slouch with the blade, and when the 'round' was completed the needle was on the red line and climbing, and as every good locomotive man knows, it was, provided there is room in the boiler, time to start the injector to prevent waste at the safety valves. In between watching the road, both my mate and I looked on approvingly. Another round was added to the fire within a few moments, after which I indicated we would soon be stopping at Brookwood. As the regulator was closed the half door was dropped, allowing more air over the top of the fire to reduce any possible excess smoke. The blower was opened slightly and a wary eye kept on the firehole door momentarily in case there was a blow back, in which case the blower would be opened further – 'poking out her tongue' could be dangerous to footplate crews. There was a repeat of this performance between each station, the water in the boiler was maintained comfortably between $^1/_2$ to $^2/_3$ of a glass of water, with just an occasional buzz from the safety valves. The longest section was the last one, Hook to Basingstoke, so it was necessary to run down the fire and allow the water to fall in the gauge glass, and this was done in good fashion.

After arrival at our destination and the train had been cleared, the shunter appeared and instructed me to set back into the 'down' sidings, London end, the ground signal was 'off' and the movement completed. My mate then placed a red tail lamp on the tender (nearside) and put up the shunting engine headcode on the front of No. 30751, white light over left buffer and a red one over the right side. The shunter next uncoupled the N15 from our train, pulled a pair of points and we moved forward to attach to a couple of vans which were to go on the rear of the 8.54pm from Waterloo to Salisbury. A brake was created, then destroyed and we now had about 45 minutes for a bite of supper etc. Armitage went to make a can of tea and Mr Hardy and I chatted. "You have done some firing in the past," I began, "only one thing was wrong this evening though, you did not perform from the proper side!" "I'm sorry Bert, I can only do it in my natural way" – which meant that when the driver was on the left side of the footplate he needed to keep out of the way of the fireman when he was performing with the blade. I hasten to add, that the 'Guv' was not on his own in this respect as I've seen LM men fire their 'Royal Scots' and 'Duchess' class locomotives from the driver's side of the footplate. I guess the main line driver's there were more tolerant of the situation than LSWR men! A fireman would quickly be told to get to his own side. As I have said before, happy is the man who can shovel with equal dexterity from either side of the footplate. The driver needed to make adjustments sometimes, for years they had driven their engines on the main line from the lefthand side of the footplate. Then, when the Maunsell N, U and U1 class 2-6-0s were introduced, the driver was on the righthand side and had to hurriedly make fresh landmarks to observe when stopping at stations and water columns. The firing technique had to be altered also, from firing level grates, often deep, to sloping ones and seldom needing coal to be thrown right to the front of the firebox. The fire would work down the firebars, especially when running hard or pulling heavily.

After the two vans were shunted onto the rear of the Salisbury train, various other small jobs turned up, such as a coach or van to be placed elsewhere etc., normal station pilot work as would be carried out at any major station on BR. Around 11.30pm we were relieved by a set of Basing men (rumour has it that when the American astronauts, Neil Armstrong and Buzz Aldrin set foot on the moon in 1969, there was a pair of Basingstoke men ready to relieve them!), who carried on pottering about whilst we repaired to the 'up' main platform to relieve a set of Salisbury men on the Sidmouth Milk, due to depart at midnight. There was always a considerable amount of shunting carried out on the rear of the train as vans and empty stock etc. were taken off and added. Usually the consist was anything from ten to twenty vehicles, often depending on how many were to be detached at Woking whilst the train stood in the station on the 'up' local line. The engine was one from Nine Elms, the exact one escapes me, I think it was an H15 – a 'Tavy Engine', formerly used by the 'Tavy gang' prior to the war when 'double-home' work was undertaken, signing off both at Exeter and Dorchester on the important freight work. Our guest had another spell on the shovel and we dropped him off at Surbiton where he lived, indicating that he had enjoyed himself and would like to come again at a future date, "Please let me know when you obtain this turn again." That was the forerunner of several trips Mr Hardy made with me on the 7.54pm to Basingstoke.

One unforgettable summer evening N15X 4-6-0 No. 32331 *Beattie*, was our engine, a rebuild from the former LBSCR Billinton 4-6-4T, 'Remembrance' class engines. The main features altered were the removal of the side and well tanks, the main frames were shortened and the coal bunker removed, the boiler pressure was increased from 170 to 180psi, the cylinders were lined up and reduced from 22in to 21in and the whole loco modified to conform to the standard SR loading gauge, to enable the class to run on all three sections. A Urie eight-wheel bogie tender was attached, resulting in a very handsome locomotive. However, the engines had a very small port on the first regulator, and they would not time three coaches when that was used, needing to get the big valve open, then they would leap forward, so the only thing to do then was to notch up to a relatively short cut-off. The sector plate was marked with seven equally placed 'bars' and the usual running place was around the second bar. If the cut-off was advanced to the third bar or just beyond when steaming hard the fire would disappear from under the door and go down the steep slope of the grate and pile up under the brick arch. Immediately there would be a falling off in boiler pressure and the fireman would be making frantic efforts with the fire irons to pull the fire back to the back end! Conversely, if the driver 'pulled her up' to about the first bar, the fire would lose its draught and the boiler would begin to wilt.

Like most 'Brighton' engines, they steamed well when the fire was thin and dancing across the front of the grate and 'stair rods' were going up the chimney, so, the 'Remembrance' class needed to be handled sensibly from either side of the footplate. Provided the fireman kept the fire well up under the door and back corners and sloped it evenly towards the front of the firebox, he would not need to throw much coal there. He merely needed to put some well broken up coal down the sides and watch the chimney. If the 'stair rods' ceased, then he was getting too much coal across the front, or possibly the driver had notched her up slightly, attempting to halt the fire throwing which the average LSWR driver hated, but ex-Brighton and Chatham men were used to it and took no notice of 'stair rods' providing no 'Oranges' were emitted, meaning fairly large lumps of burning coal. That was an entirely different matter! With the big regulator open and short cut-off working on nearly all of their work, the N15Xs rapidly became 'rough' with heavy wear in the axleboxes, apparent after only a few months out of shops.

So, with all this in mind I viewed *Beattie* and felt that Richard (as he had requested I call him now) would have another chapter to add to his experiences! Our charge for the evening run to Basingstoke was well run down, as was apparent going light to Waterloo. The general feeling was one of bad sloppiness in big end and coupling rod brasses, apart from the axleboxes. Richard had requested to do the firing as he felt at home with the butterfly type of firehole door, as was used on vast numbers of ex-LNER engines. He knew it was taboo to open the main door when on the road so the coal had to be well broken up in order for it to go through the smallish aperture, especially if it was necessary to put the shovel into the firebox to turn coal into the most important part – the back corners! A quick word of advice on the best type of fire to get the desired results was absorbed, a moment or two before starting time the fire was fettled up with the pricker, the hydrostatic lubricator was adjusted to my satisfaction, and my fireman of the day was parked on the small square of wood which was honoured with the name of 'seat'.

In the first regulator used to lift the train out of Waterloo over the points and crossings until the advanced starter was passed, *Beattie* was quite subservient, then when the big valve was opened the engine was transformed. A healthy roar up the chimney resulted in rapid acceleration and hurried adjustment of the cut-off to calm things down a bit! Richard soon sorted things out from the fireman's angle, the needle was on the red line and the exhaust injector working well. The N15X was a lively engine in every sense of the word! My mate soon found it quite impossible to remain on the seat and stood on the tender just behind the fall plate as the riding was better there. I sometimes marvelled at the way the injector steam pipes stood up to the constant battering they sustained during hard running, but they did and the injectors fed the water into the boiler at the desired rate. After observing the 40 mph service slack through Clapham Junction, No. 32331 was soon into her stride again and Wimbledon was passed at the ceiling of the 60 mph permanent speed restriction. Approaching Surbiton a 20 mph temporary speed restriction was in force and which was duly observed, enabling the 'Guv' to wave the firing shovel at his wife who was taking an evening stroll and just 'happened' to be on the high footbridge near their home station!

Once over the temporary speed restriction *Beattie* was soon into speed again, the big valve open and cut-off reduced gradually to just inside the second bar. Richard had got the measure of the firebox and was enjoying himself, the old girl really flew along to such good effect that we were at a stand in Woking 'down' local platform inside 30 minutes, as against the 31 allowed, despite a speed restriction which must have cost three minutes! There was no doubt the erstwhile Brighton L class tank could run. In the virtual quietness during the station stop at Woking I asked our guest if he would like to drive the engine to Basingstoke, indicating that I would give the necessary instructions re shutting off steam etc. The engine to be stopped on the station ramp unless I said otherwise, there were no more temporary speed restrictions to think about and I would also see all the signals. Richard jumped at the opportunity presented so we changed places and whilst he was looking back for the guard's green flag, I gave the footplate a good wash down with the coal watering hose prior to shutting off the exhaust injector (a rough engine does not lend itself to a coal free footplate during hard running.) He proved to be a capable driver, needing little prompting from me, hustling *Beattie* along from each station stop, thus allowing himself plenty of time to make a cautious approach at the succeeding point of call and stopping the train at the correct places. The platforms were of varying lengths and the exists were not in a 'standard' position so each station stop needed to be made with these small details in mind. All in all it was a most enjoyable trip. I always enjoyed a stint on the shovel and, like the majority of drivers, was able to maintain the boiler, observe all signals, cross the footplate to see if there were any emergency signals being given by the guard or platform staff as the train left the station, and also direct operations as to the driving of the engine – it is a satisfactory condition in which to be!

A Return Trip on the Great Eastern

During our supper time at Basingstoke, Richard asked me if I would like a trip out of Liverpool Street one evening, possibly to Chelmsford or even Ipswich. The engines used on those jobs were the B12s, a GER 4-6-0 with inside cylinders and reboilered by Gresley, or a Thompson B1 ("Bongo"). I did not hesitate to answer in the affirmative and within a few weeks it was arranged. We met at Waterloo station one evening and made our way to Liverpool Street station. (I well remember a wartime Nine Elms Top Link driver "Blinder" Read, remarking at Waterloo one day, "It gets more like Liverpool Street every day", as at the time the depot was supplied with hard Yorkshire coal and with several engines present belching smoke in various degrees the terminus did have a distinctly hazy appearance!) The former GE terminus smelt like a railway station, a mixture of coal, oil, soot and warm machinery and, I must add, not altogether unpleasant. The time of the train we were to board has long since eluded me but there was a '1500' at the 'sharp end'. We were expected and made welcome. I looked around with some interest, a clean footplate, two-thirds of a glass of water in the boiler, a long narrow firebox, reminding me of the Drummond 'Paddleboats', but the grate was 6in longer than a T14! The mechanical 'action' of the engine was superb, a lovely silky motion that seemed effortless, and after a while I was invited to 'try the blade'. There was plenty of room on the footplate to get the necessary swing on the shovel to throw the coal to the front of the 10ft level firegrate, a most satisfying experience, although I did find that the distance from the tender shovelling plate to the firehole door was rather too long for me. I had to take a short step to and fro, thus breaking the fireman's golden rule 'keep your feet still'. It was Richard's turn to watch me. He looked on approvingly as the coal rattled around the sides of the firebox, the fire burned more evenly than on the 'Paddleboats' on which it burnt more fiercely at the front of the grate, always the hardest to reach, especially when arms became tired.

The return trip from Chelmsford was on a B1 and I must confess the engine made a less favourable impression on me than did the '1500', being somewhat run down and consequently rather noisy. But, what I remember most vividly was the sacking stuffed into the gap between the firebox and the floorboards! Most unsightly, but the practical purpose was to prevent ashpan dust rising up to smother the crew! I hated dust, and therefore approved of the anti-dust precautions. I did have a turn on the shovel, and the run down "Bongo" had a healthy appetite for coal, as so many high mileage engines did.

An A4 to Leeds

One day, Richard asked, "Would you like a Sunday evening run to Leeds on an A4, return on the 9.50am Monday morning?" I gasped – "When?" "First Sunday in December" was the reply. I made a rapid scan of my rostered turns, on duty late on Saturday, Sunday off, then 4.30pm on Monday afternoon, it could not have worked out better! "Right then", Richard said, "Come to an early tea at home, then we will set off together to King's Cross. "Bill Hoole is on that turn, I'll write to Harold Binder to see if we can stay the night at his house and apply for our footplate passes. Of course, you'll need some overnight gear." I had met Bill at a railway society meeting of some description a few weeks previously and found him a quiet, charming man. Richard told me he was a hard runner and I looked forward to the trip very keenly.

The Sunday evening duly arrived and we found ourselves on the footplate of Bill's regular engine A4 No. 60007 *Sir Nigel Gresley*. We were introduced to the fireman, Albert Leach and were made welcome. I glanced around the fresh (to me) footplate, gauge glasses set high up on the boiler front showing half a glass of water, an unusual place for the sector plate (cut-off scale on the boiler front), and a reverser which looked uncommonly like an SR tender handbrake! A good fire had been built up under the door and around the back corners but very thin across the front of the grate and the A4 stood there very quiet and making little smoke. The tender was filled with good quality Yorkshire hard coal. When the platform signal cleared Albert cracked the blower slightly more and added some well broken up coal onto the thin spots, otherwise the fire would have been torn to pieces under a train-starting blast. It was obvious to me that Albert knew his craft, the half a glass of water told me that these King's Cross men did not desire any bother with an overfilled boiler whilst going up through the tunnels virtually off the platform ends. So, a good clean exit was made. Bill 'wound her up' whilst his mate plied his shovel to good purpose, and it was not long before *Sir Nigel* was on the red line. The exhaust injector was singing its contented song and all was well in our little world on the footplate. Once the environs of London were in the rear, Bill called to his fireman, "My turn for exercise", and they changed places, the driver proving that he could still feed the firebox in the proper manner.

It was a lovely clear evening, the signals stood out very clearly and the AWS bell was working perfectly. No. 60007 was running very sweetly on a short cut-off and wide open regulator, although the steam chest pressure gauge was not steady, fluctuating 50 or 60psi quite rapidly. It would be interesting to know exactly where the point of extraction was that the pipe leading to the steam chest gauge was situated. To me, an unsteady gauge indicated that the engine was working with a too short cut-off yet the action and riding quality belied that. I came to realise very early on that trip just what a grand machine this A4 was, and enhancement came later when I was invited to 'try the blade'. I quickly learned the knack of firing to the back corners, dipping the shovel under the baffle plate and finishing the movement with one hand! The engine certainly was not a 'miner's friend', being economical to run, and run she did, to my delight and satisfaction. Richard took his turn with the firing and Albert Leach virtually had an evening off, taking over towards the close of the journey in order to run down the fire in preparation to go on the shed at Leeds.

Richard had previously written to a driver friend, one Harold Binder, to see if he could put us up for the night. This was readily granted and so we made our way to his home for a bite of late supper, a wash and then to bed. Bill Hoole and his mate took the A4 to the depot, Farnley Junction, I think, where they were relieved and then retired to the dormitory for a night's sleep, to be ready for the 9.50am to King's Cross the following morning. Richard and Harold Binder had plenty to talk about but eventually nature won and bed was welcome. Harold was first up on the Monday morning and prepared an appetising breakfast for us, after which it was farewell and then over to the station.

On our way to the A4 at the head of the train, Richard had greetings with the driver of the tank engine which had worked in the empty stock which formed the 9.50am, obviously knowing the man, probably someone who figured in his early days on the railway at Doncaster. No. 60007 had been coupled on and the brake created, steam heat was on and all that was required was a clear road and the guard's green flag. At 9.50am both were in evidence and we were off. Richard and Albert Leach shared the firing duties until we were approaching Grantham when I was invited to do my share. The engine was steaming perfectly and Bill 'put her to it' up the bank to Stoke summit. I had gathered that we were two or three minutes down (nothing to do with our engine) and that the lost time was to be regained. That was all right as far as I was concerned, ascending the bank the A4 was going well, the exhaust injector maintaining the boiler around half a glass and I was happy. Once over the top the engine controls remained unaltered and I soon found I was shovelling coal faster. As the speed increased, which it did quite rapidly, the water was falling in the glass! I motioned to Albert to start the second injector then returned to the task in hand. I glanced outside, the telegraph poles were slipping past at unaccustomed speed. I was surely going the fastest speed of my life at that moment, almost certainly doing the magic 100 mph but in the absence of a speedometer it was impossible to verify with any accuracy. I know that was the liveliest bout of firing I had done since the 1948 Locomotive Exchanges when Jack Swain opened up 'West Country' No. 34006 *Bude* on leaving Leicester to run to Rugby, at the request of Mr Jarvis, Chief of the dynamometer car crew, "Give us a pull Jack!"

Bill Hoole's A4 could certainly run and gave the crew a smooth ride, in fact very similar to a Southern WC. Needless to say, I enjoyed the experience and I was sorry when the run finished at the 'Cross'. One thing remains very vividly in my mind and that is the smell of a hot, superheated engine when the regulator is closed and coasting is taking place. I have noticed this as more prevalent on A4s than any other class of locomotives, the smell is there (not unpleasant to me) but on the 'Blue uns' it seemed more pungent, and lasted longer.

This run to Leeds and return was the forerunner of several trips with Bill and an unforgettable trip on 'The Elizabethan' with Ted Hailstone on No. 60011 *Empire of India* when the middle piston rings disintegrated near York on the return run (well documented in *Railway World*, December 1986). Upon reflection, I would have liked to have had a run on an A4 with one of the accepted 'light' enginemen as no two drivers handled their engines in exactly the same way, although to obtain a good appreciation of the driving qualities of various enginemen one would need to know the road equally as well as the man at the regulator.

French Footplate Experiences
My wife Renée must have been an extremely tolerant person, to put up with my excursions into 'foreign' territory at times when, in all reality, I should have been at home. After all, the footplate crews spent a good deal of their time either at work, or in bed when people in normal occupations were socialising at the end of their day's work. So it was with some trepidation that I broached the subject of a real foreign trip to my 'domestic foreman'! "Richard has asked me if I would like a footplate run on a French locomotive, needing to stay over for a night or two." To my delight, I received 'the nod', quickly notifying him to go ahead with the necessary arrangements. The eagerly awaited day arrived, a visitor's passport having been obtained, I met the 'Guv' at Victoria station and boarded the Dover boat train. Formalities at both Dover and Calais were just that and soon I was looking at one of the noted Nord E class Pacifics as modernised by M. Chapelon, from ground level. Richard spoke French with very little hesitation. Unhappily, I knew not a word, but Fred White, an interpreter employed by the SNCF was on hand, a complete bi-linguist, born in Calais of English parents, Fred went to a local school where he became naturally fluent in French yet when he was

at home with his parents they spoke English so that language was learnt naturally also. Most peculiarly Fred had an unmistakable 'Brummie' accent! A competent man at his job and undoubtedly has eased many small problems with the language over the years.

Richard was greeted by Edmond Godry, a *chef mécanicien* (chief footplate inspector), obviously an old friend. We climbed aboard No. 231E9 and introductions were made all round. I was struck by the smallness of the footplate, at least the distance from the front of the tender to the boiler backhead – no need for the chauffeur (fireman) to step either way whilst shovelling coal – but there was ample width so that the five persons travelling on the footplate (allowed in France as against four in England) had a reasonable amount of room. I looked with interest at all the gauges and endeavoured to fathom out their use. The air brake one was marked out in atmospheres (roughly 15 psi) the train pipe showed '5' around 75 psi as against our normal 70 psi on the Westinghouse fitted stock, the main reservoir pressure was, as I recall, marked at '8', about 120 psi with large storage capacity as the train was single piped. The gauge also showed engine and tender brake cylinder pressure, another gauge indicated steam chest and receiver pressures, whilst one other, showing zero, turned out to be a pyrometer gauge, the first time that I had seen one! This instrument measured the amount of superheat obtained by the fireman, and indication of his capabilities. The usual water gauge glasses and boiler pressure dial was self explanatory but over the firehole door was a small hinged flap. I asked Richard its purpose, he slipped it to one side and invited me to look therein. I did so and was looking at a well cleaned tubeplate over the top of the brick arch! Quite a contrast to our engines when one had to remove the baffle plate and peer up over the brick arch, often not being able to see the small and lower smoke tubes above the brick arch.

Henri Dutertre was the mécanicien and 'Big Louis' (a grandfather!) was his fireman. A fire had been built up under the door, not too heavy and tapered off to fairly thin across the front of the wide grate. I judged the grate area was larger than that of a WC and I looked forward with keen interest to watch the work of the French footplatemen. The coal was very small, light in weight and burnt with a good heat. A pile of briquettes was stacked on the front of the tender for use, so Richard informed me, when the fire became 'rough' or needed to be built up again. The firehole was a large one, in three sections, a handle to operate it was placed either side, so whichever side was used the centre section always opened in conjunction with the outer one. Thus firing took place down one side of the box at a time, a rather cumbersome arrangement, rather like the principle of Dugald Drummond's LSWR firehole door, which, when opened acted as a baffle plate, deflecting the cold air onto the fire. The French locomotive did not have the Drummond 'half door' over which it was possible to fire with small coal, whilst the shovel was light, rather small without raised sides.

The 'right away' was given, Henri put the reversing lever into full forward gear and cracked the regulator, keeping an eye on the steam chest pressure gauge as simple working was used. Too much regulator would have caused the relief valve on the receiver to blow (at about 80 psi) which was considered poor enginemanship. The Pacific moved smoothly away with a barely audible exhaust, in fact I did not hear it with any clarity until we were ascending Caffiers Bank. Compound working was quickly adopted, firing was regular, little and often, making for easy work and the pressure gauge was close to the red line as though glued there. The small coal made plenty of smoke, even so the pyrometer gauge indicated a high superheat. No. E9 gave us a splendid ride and was in good mechanical condition, no steam blows, knocks and a nice even beat up the chimney. In fact, none of the problems associated with high mileage 'common user' engines. I had no idea just how many miles this marvellous machine had run since her last overhaul or if Henri had spent time in the 'Shops' working with the resident fitters during the overhaul, as was allowed for in their 'set up'. I understand that some mécaniciens did this work because of their love for the engines they drove. All in all a tremendous contribution to success on the road, the crews enjoyed a time regained bonus and a coal saving premium, a further incentive to get the best work from their charge. In addition extra pay was earned cleaning the engine but *not the tender*, so often that was the case, a clean loco attached to a dirty tender, so a clean one indicated a really keen crew!

When Henri applied the Westinghouse brake the amount of 'blow' he gave on the brake valve surprised me. I expected the train to come to an emergency stop. On our electric stock that would certainly have been the case, but the heavy train just slowed down nicely, Henri operated the engine and tender brake release valves so that the main braking force came from the train, apparently this was almost universal practice as it was not desirable for the engine and tender wheels to 'pick up', thus causing undesirable wheel flats – a wise precaution.

The journey to Paris was unforgettable but I must confess that I have seldom stepped down from a locomotive in such a dirty condition. I removed my shoes on the platform, one at a time and tipped out little piles of dust! Richard and myself then made our way to the Nord Hotel and registered in. I was somewhat dismayed at the thought of presenting ourselves to the receptionist in our obviously dirty condition, but to my surprise there was no reaction, it seemed as though Englishmen who travelled to Paris on French locomotives were to be tolerated, humoured, not to be upset – 'they'll go away when they're ready'! But seriously, it did appear as though such scenes were an everyday experience and the Nord Hotel staff took it all in their stride.

The following morning we were up early – a French breakfast, then to Nord station to ride on a De'Caso 'Baltic', a beautiful semi-streamlined 4-6-4 tender engine. André Duteil in charge, a very small wiry man, but

whose capabilities as a mécanicien were unsurpassed. I have never witnessed such delicate handling of a locomotive, and André really lived
with his engine. Apart from it being my first trip on a 'Baltic' it was also
my first on a locomotive fitted with a mechanical stoker. André's fireman
was not his regular one as he was on holiday. A few moments before
starting time a fire iron that looked uncommonly like a garden rake was
inserted into the firebox and what fire was in there levelled over, but not
enough to cover the grate. The blower was cracked and the stoker started. The coal was small, (a piece the size of a walnut was a 'lump'!) and it
seemed to burst into flame before it reached the fire. Care needed to be
taken otherwise too much smoke was too easily produced. I stood
behind André as the train was set in motion, no slipping of the drivers, a
lovely smooth start and soon compound working of this giant locomotive
was begun. I gave Richard the thumbs up sign across the footplate, the
centre of which was occupied by the bulk of the stoker screw, the chauffeur adjusted the firing rate according to André's driving, the steam
operated water pump was set but it was gradually 'beating the boiler'
and water crept up to half a glass. Suddenly there was a tirade from
André directed at his mate. Richard translated for me – "Water is too
high in the glass Bert!" I gasped, but then realised the gauge glasses were
high up on the boiler backhead, the steam pump was eased, not shut off,
that was only done when the regulator was closed and the injector started, to avoid cold water being pumped into the boiler, (with the regulator
closed there was no exhaust steam available to heat the pump water).
Gradually the water level fell to about an inch in the glass and André
was satisfied.

The engine rode very smoothly up to the 120 kph limit, and would
have gone much faster if allowed to but the Flaman speed recorder
would have indicated that and André would have been 'carpeted'. One
thing I remember distinctly was that when we were stopped at a junction
our mécanicien climbed down immediately and *ran* to the telephone on
the signal post! (no waiting here for three minutes – London area, and
five minutes country area). The journey to Chaumont passed all too
quickly. If ever I regretted not knowing any part of the French language
it was on that visit to France. One loses so much through being unable to
communicate properly. André was in the same position when he rode
with me on a 'West Country' to Bournemouth. I invited him to restart
the train away from Woking on the 'down' trip, and his sensitive fingers
almost caressed the regulator, but he had the train moving without an
atom of slipping. No need to speak on that occasion but when I made an
indication to 'pull her up' André would not touch the steam reverser, so
I made the necessary adjustments.

I made several trips to France through the courtesy of Richard and the
Chief of M.P. – M. Leroy. Richard and myself were with Henri on
No. 231K82. I had requested to do the firing, which was readily given, as
I wanted to see how high I could get the superheat. The text books state

that high superheat comes with a clear chimney, but K82 disproved that theory. I fired that engine 'little and often', paid due regard to the back corners and the pyrometer gauge climbed to maximum when the chimney was smoking like an ocean liner! Later on in the run Richard informed me that we were approaching a PW slack of 50kph and as we were running at just over 60kph I wondered how Henri would slow the train, to give the Westinghouse Brake sufficient train pipe reduction to ensure the triple valves functioned properly throughout the 14-car train would mean our speed dropping right down, possibly to 25kph. I witnessed enginemanship of high order, the regulator was almost closed, about 20 psi in the steam chest, and on the side of the cab were three small valves as on a bugle. These were the dry sand valves which were operated for a few seconds, a 'carpet' of sand appeared under the driving wheels and the train perceptibly slowed! It was all judged to a nicety, down to 50 kph at the commencement of the slack. A little more steam was applied to keep at the 50 mark until the termination was reached, then normal work was resumed. I remarked to Richard, "You can learn something every day on this job!"

On one occasion I went across the Channel in company with my good friend George Barlow, then foreman driver on the 15-inch gauge Romney, Hythe & Dymchurch Railway. George was not a good sailor, had a small bout of mal-de-mer and felt distinctly unsteady as we walked to the locomotive. I'm not sure if it was an E or G, but whatever, its effect on George was beneficial. He was back to normal by the time we had surmounted the Caffiers Bank some 20 miles from Calais and settled down to enjoy his trip to Paris. The next morning, after a night in the Nord Hotel again, we set off for the short walk to the Gare de L'Est to board the 0740 to Troyes engine No. 231K70. We were not expected as the mécanicien was just closing the cab doors. I climbed the steps, "Bonjour m'sieur" – he reopened the cab door and we shook hands. George followed and greeted the crew in similar manner. I handed our joint footplate permit to the driver who examined it curiously. He beamed and made us welcome, and handing back the permit he introduced himself as M. Baton and his chauffeur M. Garcia, who immediately asked us if we "parlez-vous Spanish, Dutch, German or Italian?" Unhappily we had to answer, "Non". With the initial pleasantries over it was starting time and M. Baton exercised the same care in getting the train moving. Compound working was quickly adopted and K70 soon proved she was no slouch, and once clear of the environs of Paris speed was soon up to the maximum 120kph and we were racing over nice level track.

I made motions to the fireman indicating I would like to fire the engine, he presented the shovel to me with a flourish and promptly sat down on some briquettes and proceeded to twiddle his thumbs! George joined in the general laughter and I got on with the pleasure of firing this superb loco, and within a few moments George was invited to sit on the mécanicien's seat, somewhat like a bicycle seat on a sprung pillar, whilst our host sat on some briquettes and pretended to go to sleep! What an amazing crew, George called out to me "I shall wake up in a minute Bert. I've dreamt that I was driving a French Pacific across Northern France and old Bert Hooker was firing it!" "It's no dream George", I replied. "Enjoy the moment". All too soon we arrived at Troyes, where engines were changed.

We were sorry to leave the company of M'sieurs Baton and Garcia, but our new engine was No. 231K83 from Troyes to Vesoul. I'm unhappy to record the atmosphere on the fresh footplate was completely different. The mécanicien was a very young man and I had the feeling he had but recently taken charge of a main line engine, and footplate guests, especially foreigners, were not exactly welcome. Mécanicien Marais' chauffeur – M. Puthois however was the most relaxed fireman I have ever encountered. He stood up to the comparative thrashing meted out to the K83 well, as for the first time I heard a French locomotive making really audible exhaust noises up the chimney for long periods. I hasten to add that I had no idea of the gradients on the line so heavy working of the engine may have been necessary to keep time. We stopped at a station and took water, while our young driver *ran* around the engine and tender, underneath as well, as it was over a pit, and felt every bearing! We had a welcome break at Vesoul and made use of the time in the refreshment room to fortify ourselves for the return journey, the 13.47 to Cheamont.

The train rolled in, an enormous 241A, Mountain locomotive on the front, number A27. We climbed aboard, showed the permit and were made welcome. The footplate was quite short, and the fireman had a comfortable position for firing – he needed to have, as the firebox was hand fired, although a coal pusher was provided so that coal was always available for use. George estimated the smokebox was about a quarter of a mile away when he peered through the spectacle glass! Once again we were hampered by lack of language knowledge but there was no doubt mécanicien Jean Demougeot and chauffeur Jean Robin of Chaumont depot were masters of their craft. No. 241A27 was a good locomotive with a good turn of speed despite hauling a long, heavy train. I was fascinated with the handling of the true Westinghouse single pipe brake. Only air pumps and reservoir on the locomotive, and misuse of the brake could easily lead to trouble as the whole system needed to be recharged with air before the brake is effective again, which does not happen almost simultaneously!

Engines were changed again at Cheaumont, and we bade farewell to our competent hosts and transferred to a similar locomotive, No. 241A8, in the charge of M. Jean Sabozde and M. Henri Bertrand. As the footplate fittings were polished No. A8 was obviously their 'own' engine, but again, I was to see the peculiar French practice of not cracking the blower whilst standing at stations, consequently smoke and flames seeped out from the closed firehole doors and got out through the cab roof ventilator, soiling the clean brass and steel in the process. And of course, smoke just rolled out of the chimney, sufficient to make our loco inspectors tear their hair if it happened in England! Arrival in Paris was right time, the time passing all too quickly on this magnificent locomotive, the riding qualities of which were little different to the Pacifics. The following day our train from Paris Nord to Calais was double headed. Running at reduced speed as per regulation, and easy work for the locomotives, and I must confess it was the least interesting journey I made on a French footplate.

Electrification was taking over, so I was able to sample the new electric locomotive between Amiens and Paris Nord. Very powerful machines with a tremendous acceleration. The "Americanos" were tried also, the ex-U.S. Army 141Rs, strong, hard riding engines but just what did the French crews really think of them after their marvellous compounds? After a hundred or so miles at being thumped and thrown about they must have sighed for the more gentle qualities of the E&G Pacifics.

I have splendid memories of French locomotives and their capable crews, and how I would have loved to have driven one on our main lines, with a tender full of good Welsh 'cauliflower' coal. Economical? I should say. Impossible of course as the 231Es would have fouled our loading gauge, plus the fact that a vacuum brake ejector would have to be fitted, although that would not have been insurmountable. It's nice to dream! I never saw a chauffeur handle the regulator and always in my memory is Edmond Godry, 'Chief mécanicien', who gently chided me on one occasion, "Bébert, mécaniciens no fire!" On my journeys I have looked at the train, often over 600 tons, looked at the coal the fireman was burning, not in vast quantities either, and I have thought 'La Belle Machines indeed'. We have some way to go to catch up!

During my main line years at Nine Elms, Richard rode with me many times, but to his disappointment never on a 'Paddleboat' as they had all gone by the time I knew him. Nor on an H15 'City class' Nos 330 to 335, only once on a 'Nelson' on the 7.54pm to Basingstoke, so his trips with me were on Bulleid Pacifics in original condition and rebuilt, on which he provided plenty of good hot steam, proving he was master of our craft.

The BR Standard 5s were ridden on also. On one unforgettable day he brought along Mr R. Jennings, one time House Master and Registrar at Marlborough College, to ride from Basingstoke to Bournemouth on MN No. 35003 *Royal Mail*, and return on BR class 5 No. 73037. Reginald and his wife Miriam were charming people and I spent many pleasant hours in their company at their home in Salisbury whilst awaiting my return train on the occasions I have a 'Sarum' turn. I would telephone them on the day previous to the job and thus be met at the station – wonderful times, made possible by the fact that on 'Warship' hauled trains one had about two hours awaiting the return service, without the necessity of going to 'Loco' to perform engine requirements, as in the steam engine era.

4

Steam Specials

THE RUNNING OF special trains, from Christmas mails and parcel trains to boat trains, along with railway club and society tour specials, has always interested me. In particular the latter were of interest as locomotives ventured over routes where they were not normally to be seen. Then, as the societies became more ambitious, requests were made of BR for the temporary transfer of engines from one region to another to have train loads of railway enthusiasts who delighted in being drawn along by a 'foreign' locomotive. By and large, BR responded well to these unusual requests during the final ten years or so of steam traction. In fact once a special train, organised by a society had been sanctioned from HQ the clerks delegated to do the inter-regional arrangements entered into the spirit of the thing. The tours were therefore usually well organised, but there were some of course, when things went awry, and engines have been known to run out of coal or steam. But generally, the loco crews acquitted themselves well, to the satisfaction of the tour organisers, who often chose a most suitable and appropriate name for the trains.

After the 1948 Loco Exchanges, I was soon rostered on Nine Elms Goods Yard and, being ambitious to get some running work, I seized the opportunity to go on to the Dual Panel when two or three vacancies were advertised. I think there were about a dozen drivers on the Panel with quite senior men thereon down to passed firemen. Five or six Sunday electric traction duties were allocated to Nine Elms and the nearest Panel man on his own roster would be booked the turn and his own duty would be covered by spare men in the normal way. The Panel was also a spare pool for weekday electric jobs when they were unable to be covered by motormen – the electrical department did not have many spare drivers to cover sickness, etc., so to see a Panel man in overalls on electric work caused few eyebrows to rise!

I figured that once I had learned all the third rail lines out of Waterloo, (which consisted of all the inner suburban, Horsham, Alton, Reading and Portsmouth lines) any steam specials which cropped up – and I had signed the road, could well be in line for me to get the work. The Pompey road was considered to be 'main line', but as the Pilot Gang had no rostered work over the route, only two or three of the drivers were able to keep in touch with it due to the Dual Panel.

The day I was appointed as a driver at Nine Elms, I was booked to begin Electrical Training at London Bridge station. The instructor was a former LBSC guard, one of the original 'half-a-crown men', as mentioned in Chapter 1. Anyway, our instructor was a knowledgeable and likeable person, and I was soon into the world of fuses, knife switches, resistances and the Westinghouse brake, the three weeks training period finished and our Chief Roster Clerk, Fred Wilde, indicated that six weeks was the standard period in which to learn all electric roads! Due to firing over the inner suburban lines on short road goods in my early days at the Premier Depot I was familiar with them. The important thing when on electric traction was to know just where your four car gaps were, so I was more able to concentrate on learning Horsham, Alton, Reading and Portsmouth. If one felt that more time was needed for road learning, a further two weeks would be allocated – so, in those days it paid to ride with a motorman who was able to pass on his knowledge and know how in willing fashion. Alternatively one could seek out a former Nine Elms colleague who had gone to Waterloo or Wimbledon Park depots for promotion to driver during the war. The Foremen Motormen at Waterloo were always helpful in this respect.

The 'West Surrey Special'
In 1952 I was in the Railway Correspondence and Travel Society (RCTS), a thriving concern that organised many rail tours. On reading through the society journal, *The Railway Observer*, I saw that a special train was to be run from Waterloo to Victoria via East Putney, Brookwood, Camberley, Ascot, Twickenham, Clapham Junction, Stewarts Lane then into Victoria. The engine requested was an Adams 0395 class 0-6-0 freight loco. I checked my roster and found I was on duty Sunday, 23rd November, the date of the tour, and as I had signed for the entire route except Clapham Junction to Victoria, I thought I would write to Bert Hurst, then Secretary of the RCTS suggesting that he request my services for the 'West Surrey' special. What better than having a Society member at the regulator? The somewhat unusual request was readily granted and I found myself booked on at 2pm 'spare' on the Saturday prior to the day of the tour. As there were no 0395 class engines shedded at Nine Elms, one was sent up from Guildford during Friday evening and it stood outside No. 4 road, dead. I went in to see the R/F on duty and asked, "Have you got anything lined up for me?" He replied in the negative, so I went on, "In that case you won't mind if I put in a couple of hours on 30577, I've got her on that special tomorrow morning." "You go ahead Bert," he replied, "I know where you are if I should need you."

I deposited my bag in the cabin, went to my locker and donned a set of old overalls, then to the stores to borrow a handbrush, torch lamp, firing shovel and a wire brush. I intended to make sure, as far as possible that the 0395 would not be short of steam on what would be a long trip, as after all, the engine did not normally go very far outside a ten-mile radius of Guildford. On arrival on the loco, I removed the baffle plate, noting with satisfaction that it was a new one. The torch lamp was lit and placed near the fire hole door, my tools were deposited in the firebox and in I went, feet first. Then, reaching out for the flare lamp, this was placed on the brick arch, or what there was of it, about four rows of bricks. 'There won't be much of a reservoir of heat there', I thought. The wire brush was now put to good use, cleaning the firebox walls and crown sheet. Iron pyrites in some coals have a tendency to build up and form small stalactite formations which would absorb heat and on the tube plate would hinder the passage of the heat through the tubes. The rubbish was readily removable, the brick arch was brushed off and now the firing shovel came into use, to remove the residue of clinker which had been left in the back corners and under the door. As the firebox was deep, the straight fire irons could not reach that part of the grate so there was usually a modicum of clinker left under the door. The clinker was thrown out onto the footplate and I made a mental note to make sure my fireman raked out the ashpan prior to leaving the shed on Sunday morning.

Satisfied that the firebox was clean I next turned to the smokebox. The door had been drawing air as the inner plate was burnt at the bottom, so some grease was applied on the asbestos sealing ring, hoping that it would help it to do its job. The petticoat in the chimney was given a couple of clumps to dislodge any soot and dirt and examination of the interior revealed that it was hanging true over the blast pipe, on the top of which reposed an oily deposit resembling battlements. This was soon removed, an old screwdriver cleared the holes in the blower ring which was now roughly on the level with the top of the blast pipe. The smoke tubes appeared to be reasonably clean, and with the firehole door open it was possible to peer through a good number of them. With the fireman's side of the preparation completed I turned my attention to the driver's work. Locating the correct size spanner and some paraffin I laid on my stomach in the motions, removed the big ends and eccentric tops across the axle, extracted the trimmings and cleaned them in the paraffin. They were in surprisingly good condition, but then Guildford always had a good reputation for looking after the engines at the depot. After the trimmings had been replaced I topped up the reservoirs with oil, noting the corks were in good condition. The small ends, slide bar oil boxes, piston gland cups and trimmings were dealt with next, followed by the coupling rods and tender axleboxes. That was as far as I could go with the preparation, but I was pleased with the work thus performed. I was confident old 30577 would run and steam satisfactorily – now for a wash and some tea.

On Sunday morning I booked on with my fireman of the day, Jim Sullivan, a main line man for which I was thankful. The engine and tender had been wiped down and she looked quite presentable in BR black. Jim and I had a chat abut the job, as it was as strange to him as it was to me to have an 0395 on a passenger turn. Previously our experience of the class had been confined to shunting work in Wimbledon and Raynes Park goods yards. We went about the engine preparation after I had appraised Jim of the work completed the previous day. His eyebrows shot up but he offered no comment, then he built up a good fire under the door whilst I completed the necessary oiling, paying particular attention to the steam brake. The boiler was pressed at 150psi but the Ramsbottom safety valves began to blow at 140, blowing off hard at 145! The injectors were tried, no problems there and the dry sand ran freely under the leading wheels. Jim raked out the ashpan when we were on the pit prior to topping up the coal.

As we were about to leave the depot, Arthur Langdon, Chief Locomotive Inspector climbed aboard. I had expected to see an inspector, hoping it would be Albert Plummer, but not the 'Chief'. Anyway, we made our way to Waterloo and Jim coupled on to seven coaches, some of them articulated, another request I think from the RCTS. No steam heat from our end as No. 30577 was not so fitted, after all, it was late November and surely the Society organisers would be aware of the fact, so I hoped the loco crew who worked the ingoing empties had given the train a good 'bake-up' for a start. I remarked to my mate, "No steam heat won't make a deal of difference as the chaps will have the windows down anyway!", and so it proved.

The great ex LSWR terminus was left on time at 12.38pm, down the Windsor local line. The 0395s had enormous reversing levers, and with full first regulator it was impossible for someone of my small stature to adjust the cut-off. Most drivers closed the regulator to 'pull her up', then re-opened up, usually causing a jerk in the train. This I disliked to do, so I adjusted the regulator until there was just a breath of steam passing through, grasped the reversing lever which was 'in the corner', and judged the time to put the lever in the third notch. I then opened the regulator on to the first full port, and happily, all was completed very smoothly. The boiler pressure had fallen to 120psi and I noticed the brake ejector was ticking and the train pipe needle was unsteady. Jim had seen it also so he reached for the pricker to liven up the fire and the boiler soon responded with train pipe vacuum remaining steady at 21in – the ejector cones probably needed cleaning. All this revealed that we had at most a 25psi margin, just below 120 the brakes would begin to leak on along the train. Above 140psi the safety valves were blowing, so Jim would need to watch points quite closely if we were to have a successful trip. Up the short sharp bank from Wandsworth Town to East Putney I ventured to put the regulator right over, and with about two-thirds of a glass of water No. 30577 did not prime, which augured well for the heavy banks to come later in the trip.

Once out on the main line at Wimbledon, the 0395 ambled along at around 40mph, touched 45 near Weybridge (still in the 3rd notch) and I tried the second one, but the engine was not happy there. On level and slightly down hill running the first regulator sufficed, on rising ground the big valve was just broken, which kept the speed somewhat constant. Jim soon arranged his firing so that after he had added a round to the fire, he would pull up the sliding doors, the boiler made steam and with the pressure rising he started the injector. This gradually 'beat the boiler', adding more water than was being used, so the level in the glass rose, and when the steam fell back to 125/130 psi the injector was shut off and firing followed. By this means water was maintained at a comfortable $\frac{1}{2}$ to $\frac{3}{4}$ glass and boiler pressure just below blowing off. Our arrival at Brookwood heralded a little activity. We had to unhook and run light engine back to Woking Up Yard to replenish the water tank and to refill the lubricator on the smokebox side, and oil the 'links and glands'. A can of tea was made and drunk with our sandwiches, then a return to Brookwood. In the meantime the train had gone on to the Bisley Tramway hauled by an M7 0-4-4 tank in charge of Guildford men. This was the last passenger train to traverse the Tramway. On our restart, we went down the local line to Sturt Lane Junction, turned off to the right through Frimley Junction, then through Frimley and the line steepened approaching Camberley, through that station and we were on a 1 in 60 gradient! At the foot of the gradient the water was creeping up the glass. I asked Jim to shut off the injector and for the first time on the journey the inspector gave voice on the running of the locomotive. "Leave the feed on", he directed, and Jim did so. Consequently, when I opened the regulator on to the big valve, old 30577 primed badly, a fount of water gushed up the chimney, taking the cylinder lubrication with it. I was not very pleased and probably showed it.

I had to close the regulator, losing momentum on the bank, the priming ceased and I opened the regulator again on to the first valve. My mate had shut off the injector, I pushed the regulator handle again into the big valve, and now that the old girl had rid herself of the excess water she was happy to 'dig in' with the job in hand. But now I realised the lever, in its present position, in the third nick, would not be enough to surmount the 1 in 60. If I knocked out the catch holding the lever in the third nick it would go forward violently, doubtless causing the boiler to prime again, and we could have caused ourselves some problems, perhaps even stalling. In anticipation of needing to advance the cut-off with the regulator wide open I had a large spanner handy. I placed it in the fifth notch, gave the catch a hearty knock and the lever went forward to come up short against the spanner – just the right amount to enable our little engine to sail up the 1 in 60 – to the short tunnel at the top of the gradient. The sparks were flying all right up the chimney, but I did not think that LSWR locos could throw their fire like that!

There was sufficient water in the glass for ample safety as we turned the top of the bank, and I shut off to coast down a similarly steep gradient to Bagshot, which lay at the bottom of a dip in the road. Whenever I was on electric train duties over the line I always called at Bagshot and have always wanted to run through the place. Now it was happening. The chaps timing the train agreed we reached 61 mph through Bagshot station! Surely, No. 30577 had never turned her wheels at that speed in her 45-odd years of work! But, she ran sweetly and relatively quietly, and going out of the dip from Bagshot I let her run out until speed fell to about 35 mph. I then re-adjusted the cut-off to the 3rd notch and, with the first regulator open, we jogged along preparing to reduce speed to 20 mph for the curve into Ascot. All signals were 'off' and once clear of the platform, the 'big valve' was used to get us up the short sharp rise to Drake and Mounts. Over the summit I shut off, put the lever in full forward and let her coast down through Sunningdale and Virginia Water. We had the road and I was reliably informed 30577 touched 58mph at Egham, roughly at the foot of the long slope from Drake and Mounts. All the hard work and running was now over apart from the gradual rise from Ashford up to Feltham, but 30577 game to the last, still responded to Jim's work with the shovel. Easy work up through Richmond and so to Clapham Junction where we were joined by a Stewarts Lane driver for the last leg into Victoria. As I had no idea of the road to that terminus the Stewarts Lane man took charge and within ten minutes or so the tour was over. I felt the bearings and to my relief the old girl had run cold, although I did note that the smokebox door was glowing at the bottom, evidence of hard work. The empty stock was worked away and we followed light engine to Clapham Junction, where our pilotman left us, as did the inspector. A few more moments and we were under the column in Nine Elms Loco, and as our day was up we were relived by a disposal crew. Several years afterwards, Danny Knight (our 1948 Exchanges Inspector) told me that at a Trains Meeting the following morning, presided over by Mr T. E. Chrimes, M. P. Officer, he was asked how the 'West Surrey Rail Tour' had gone. Mr Chrimes informed the tour had been a success, speeds reached were 61 mph at Bagshot and 58 at Egham, and his comment was, "Good heavens! What was young Hooker thinking about?"

RCTS 25th Anniversary Special

The RCTS celebrated the first 25 years of existence in 1953 and to mark the occasion a special train to Exeter was organised. A Drummond D15 4-4-0 express passenger engine was requested from Waterloo to Salisbury and one of the great engineers' T9s on to Exeter. I was Sunday off on that day and as there was plenty of work around in those days if one volunteered to work an 'extra' Sunday, a turn was usually forthcoming. However, on this occasion I did not do so but went in to see the 'Guvnor' – Mr Gilchrist, to see if there was any possibility of getting booked on the special. "I'm afraid not. If I book you on that turn, I'll get all sorts of complaints as it will be a mileage job and an early turn at that, so if you want the turn you will have to see the driver who is booked on it in the normal way and ask him if he doesn't mind you working for him as an agreed substitute". I anticipated that answer but there was no harm in trying! When the Sunday alteration sheet was posted I scanned it to see who was booked on the RCTS special, and it was my friend Jerry Sartin. What a stroke of luck. I went to his home near Vauxhall station to be greeted thus, "Give me the changeover note Bert, you're welcome to that job tomorrow!" I hastily wrote the c/o note, we both signed it and I returned to Nine Elms virtually 'walking on air' and presented it to the Roster Clerk, Mr Parsons. There were not many drivers who would give away such a Sunday duty and I was always indebted to Jerry for his kindness to me, a young driver. I must say that he was an exemplary engineman and his firemen must have found it a joy to fire to him – I know I would have, but never had the opportunity.

So, the job was mine and I booked on in good time on Sunday morning with Jerry's mate Jim Hawkins, to prepare the engine in the normal manner this being No. 30464, a D15. She had been on a Lymington turn on the previous day, had not been cleaned and there was no opportunity to give the engine a thorough check as I had done on No. 30577. The D15s had Walschaerts gear on two inside cylinders, not exactly a common arrangement, and there were plenty of corks in the motions to remove and replace after filling each reservoir with engine oil. It was a vastly different task than oiling engines such as the Maunsell N and U class 2-6-0s with their Walschaerts valve gear on the outside. The oiling was completed, during which time Jim had seen to his part in the business, fire made up, sandboxes checked, ashpan checked etc. Next, it was down to No. 1 pit road to take water and top up with coal, then up to Waterloo, but so far I had not seen an inspector. Then there was Danny Knight on the platform, who watched Jim couple on to the train. I descended to the platform to take charge of the RCTS brass rimmed headboard used for their rail tours, only to be curtly instructed to get back onto the footplate and, "get your brake". I did so and the society official gave the headboard to Jim, who included it in the classic headcode of 'top and middle bottom' – Waterloo to Plymouth. The brake was created, the guard tested it and came up to the footplate – "Seven on driver, 245 tons, nothing short to Salisbury", meaning Salisbury first stop. I asked the inspector if he was going to ride with us and he answered in the negative, so I guess we were somewhat relieved. The job always seemed to go better when there was just the driver and his mate on the footplate.

Departure from No. 14 platform was down the Windsor local line from Waterloo, crossing over to the 'down' main through, on the advance starter, usually a lengthy business so we were well on our way before the D15 could be opened up. The ten inch piston valves could deliver plenty of steam to the 19$\frac{1}{2}$in x 26in cylinders and adjustment to the cut-off was made with the Drummond steam reverser. This was operated by a single small lever over the cut-off indicator, the pulling of the same right back opened the steam valve which fed into a cylinder. A piston contained therein was coupled to the weighbar shaft, and as the piston moved the shaft moved upward, shortening the travel of the piston valves, thereby reducing the amount of steam admitted to the cylinders and allowing expansion to take place. When the cut-off indicator had reached the desired spot the operating lever was moved to the central position, the catch dropped into its slot and, provided the reverser hydraulic cylinder was filled with the correct grade of oil, and the washers are oil-tight, the hydraulic cylinder would hold the cut-off steady. If the latter were not in good condition the reverser would not hold up and the lever would creep forward, lengthening the cut-off, consequently using more steam, water and coal! An undesired objective.

When No. 30464 began to get a move on the exhaust beat began to become more throaty, a glance at the cut-off indicator revealed that the lever was advancing to the 40 per cent from the previously desired 30 per cent, back came the operating lever again, the indicator registered 30 per cent then 25 per cent and at 20 per cent the exhaust beat softened considerably, telling me that was as high as she wanted to be. Central position again for the small lever but to no avail and after a few moments the cut-off was advancing again. To my displeasure and Jim's concern, as it would be difficult to maintain a somewhat constant steaming rate, which does help an intelligent fireman, there was nothing for it but to attempt to hold the gear up with steam. This was a delicate operation but it could be done, the Drummond reversers were sluggish affairs and I have known delays to be caused by the reversers being stuck in the middle (mid gear) when reversing has been attempted with a steam chest full of steam. The cylinder drain cocks should have been opened to release the steam prior to reversing when unable to start, and enginemen have even shut off the hydrostatic lubricator to avoid a build up of steam in the slide valve steam chest, and had the heavy fire iron (dart) in between the driving wheels to lever the gear upwards and backwards. But though the Bulleid and Stirling reversers would reverse the engine against an open regulator they could not be held up with steam. So the apparatus on our D15 did have its virtues and in between watching the road and signals I managed to keep the loco running sweetly and Jim Hawkins contented. The D15's were grand engines, known by some of the old drivers as "piston valve Bulldogs", but they were rather superior to the L12s which were always known as "Bulldogs". No. 30464 was a good engine, past her prime, but even so, was capable of running express trains with moderate loads. The class had a reputation of being economical on coal and water and with ample grate area, albeit a sloping one, so they were a 'snip' to fire. We reached a speed of 78mph through Andover and another similar speed near Porton, the engine riding well at those speeds. I enjoyed the trip, although it was unfortunate that the steam reverser was not in first class condition, otherwise more attention could have been made to slightly bettering the general running and perhaps reaching the road speed limit of 85 mph. The RCTS chaps were pleased with the run however. After arrival at Salisbury, Jim unhooked and we departed for Salisbury Loco to turn the engine and take loco requirements prior to running back light engine to Nine Elms Loco – a pleasing day's work. The 'Anniversary Special' carried on to Exeter behind T9 No. 30711 and gave the passengers some really fine running over the switchback LSWR main line.

A Brighton Atlantic to Guildford

On 6th February 1955, the RCTS again organised another ambitious rail tour using a Brighton Atlantic, two Brighton E5X 0-6-2 tanks and a T9. I hasten to add, not all coupled together, although the two tankies ran coupled bunker to bunker for their part of the journey. However, I was only really interested in the first part of Waterloo to Guildford via Brentford and Chertsey. My mate for the day was Bill Botten who had had firing experience on the Atlantics, probably the only fireman at Nine Elms at the time who had done so. The only experience I had of the class was preparing and disposing of them as a cleaner and as spare fireman at New Cross Gate. Even so, that was something as against not even having climbed onto the footplate! But any engineman worth his salt, would soon find out the capabilities of a strange engine, and the injectors would be of primary importance along with the engine brake.

So Bill and I walked along Wandsworth Road from Nine Elms to Stewarts Lane depot and reported to the R/F on duty. Mr R. H. N. Hardy was shedmaster there at the time, a few months before he moved on to promotional pastures. He was in the R/F's office and greeted me, "Have you come over for the Atlantic Special Bert? I wondered if you might get that job." I answered in the affirmative, pleased to see the 'Guvnor'. The foreman went on, "Your engine is 32421, she's over a pit near the hopper." Mr Hardy said, "I'll see you again before you go." Bill and I went to our steed, and found she had been cleaned and looked very good in BR black, but not as good, I thought, as in SR Maunsell olive green. We checked the tools, they were all there, Bill applied the blower and peered into the firebox, the tubeplate was clean and there were no leaks. I said I would check the ashpan when I had oiled the valve gear underneath, the blower was eased off and we went about the normal preparation duties. Bill made a start by attending to the Westinghouse brake pump underneath the smokebox, lubricating it properly and making sure the steam cylinder drain cocks were open, then carefully opening the steam cock on the footplate to start the pump. When the water had cleared he closed the drain cocks and it began to thump away in a healthy manner. If the pump stopped whilst out on the road it was a foolhardy business to go along the gangway framing to the front of the loco to give the pump a clump with a spanner to re-start it! So a reliable air pump was a necessity, if that stopped unnoticed and the air was lost there was only the tender handbrake to halt progress when running light engine. A 'Brighton' man subconsciously listened for his Westinghouse pump to keep working!

The tender tank was topped up, but as there was adequate coal on the tender there was no need to visit the coal hopper, after all, we were only going to run about 35 miles. A Loco Inspector, George Bollen, joined us as we were about to leave. Mr Hardy came over and wished he was going with us, and George said, "You are welcome if you have a foot-plate pass". Unhappily one was not forthcoming and so we left the 'Lane', engine first to Clapham Junction, Kenny Sidings, reversed to travel up the Windsor local line to Waterloo and on to our train in No. 12 platform, which was somewhat overcrowded with enthusiasts. One of the RCTS members, one Clive Dunkley, whom I had known for several years, spoke to me, "There's been a lot of ticket applications and the load has been increased to ten coaches. Will you be alright on the Byfleet curve under the main line and up on to the down local line?" I assured him that we would. Clive went on, "They are a bit concerned up there" – a wave of his arm indicating the offices facing on to the con-course – "that you may stall on the Byfleet curve." I already had my approach to that possible problem lined up and I re-assured my friend that 'we would be all right'. By this time, Bill had coupled on, I created a brake, 21in of vacuum showing steady. George opened the Jackson valve, whereby the engine and tender air brake was applied proportion-ately with the vacuum brake. I slipped off the engine, away from the platform side, to check that the coach brake pistons were right down – two coach lengths I walked, and all the brakes were off. Satisfied, I returned to the footplate, but I did not want a dragging brake just for the sake of pulling a few strings. The guard gave me the load, "10 on for 360 tons". The presence of the Atlantic certainly created a stir at Waterloo. I'm not sure if one worked out during the ill-starred Farnborough Air Show week of a few years previously (1950), when ex-GE airbraked stock was used. If not, then the last previous occasions were when Basingstoke Loco 'inherited' some Brighton 4-4-2s for some of their passenger work to London during the early years of the war.

Waterloo was left right time and I did not intend to make a fuss with slipping and the accompanying pyrotechnics, so we eased our way over the maze of points from No. 12 platform to the 'down' Windsor Local line. Once over Westminster Bridge, I opened up No. 32421 *South Foreland* a bit, adjusted the cut-off with the aid of the air assisted reverser, a touch of the big regulator and the old Atlantic began to dig in. At Queen's Road, we were put on to the fast line and so were able to dash through Clapham Junction without reducing speed. On the local line, speed would have had to be reduced to 25 mph. Progress was good through Barnes and on to the Hounslow Loop, but when we arrived at Feltham Junction we were stopped to allow various 'up' and 'down' Reading and Windsor services to pass. Eventually, we had the road and swept along through Feltham, the Atlantic riding well and giving us a smooth ride. I was impressed and thought this will probably be the only occasion the line will see a Brighton Atlantic. The

20mph permanent speed restriction through Staines and over the River Thames was observed, past the crossings of Thorpe Lane, Egham Causeway and Pooley Green. Egham distant signal dropped off and so we were able to get a run up the bank to Virginia Water where we turned off left on to the Chertsey line. There was another 20 mph through the turn off and station, then down the bank to Chertsey. All signals were 'off' and we were approaching Addlestone and the same named junction just beyond, whose signal was at caution. I slowed right down, the home was lowered, then the starter – the Atlantic moving about 10 mph. I had advanced the lever to about 50 per cent cut-off with just a breath of steam going through the cylinders. All eyes on the distant signal for Byfleet Junction, two or three hundred yards from it and it dropped 'off', full first regulator, then a touch of the big valve and 32421 jumped to it, down hill past the distant, under the main line, then we were going uphill on a right-hand curve onto the 'down' local line. The old girl seemed to swoop around the curve and as the train entered it, it perceptively slowed as the gradient and flange drag took their toll. Full regulator now but she 'had them' and emerged triumphantly onto the 'down' local line. My mate had done his stuff, the Ramsbottom safety valves were buzzing and the water was kept well in sight in the gauge glass. He certainly had the knack of getting the coal into the back corners of the wide Wootton firebox, and pressure soon falls if the back corners are not fed.

Progress was now normal for an Atlantic hauling ten coaches of train enthusiasts along the gently rising gradients through Byfleet to Woking where we turned off on the 20 mph turn off onto the Portsmouth main line. One last sprint down through Worplesdon and I asked Bill if he needed any help to run down the fire ready for disposal in Guildford Loco. If he had too much on I could extend 32421 up the 1 in 111 gradient after Worplesdon and burn off the excess, but I was assured the fire was, "just right". I was not surprised, but more than pleased with the answer. Bill had turned off the steam heat to the train and we glided in through the long 20 mph turnout into Guildford station, the brake was destroyed, vacuum small jet closed, George re-adjusted the Jackson valve whilst Bill unhooked. The RCTS headboards were removed to be replaced onto the leading engine of the double-header which was to take over the train. Uncoupling completed, the shunt signal was 'off' and we moved forward into the tunnel, a touch on the whistle, the signalman reversed the road and we went into the Loco. "Save a fire" the R/F instructed. I checked around *South Foreland*, and confirmed she had run cold, whilst Bill got on with the disposal chores. I ruminated upon my only trip on an Atlantic tender engine and realised just what a grand engine No. 32421 was, completely vindicating all that my cousin Ern King of Newhaven shed had told me about them. He had both fired and driven them on the Newhaven boat trains and other passenger work and maintained they were "an engine and a half"! Despite their big cylinders,

21in x 26in stroke the engines were not over cylindered, as the boiler was large with adequate grate area. A big boiler was always an asset.

An Ian Allan Special to Eastleigh

On 20th April 1955, Ian Allan organised a special train from Victoria to Eastleigh via Clapham Junction, Staines, Ascot and Camberley, joining the main line at Sturt Lane Junction. A Drummond T9 4-4-0 express passenger engine had been requested, hauling eight Maunsell corridor coaches, quite a challenge for a moderately sized loco nearing the end of its working life. I approached the R/F, Ted Eatwell and his assistant Arthur Jupp, with whom I had been cleaning at New Cross Gate, re the special. My roster was 6am shunting on Nine Elms Goods and the turn was covered by a driver from the main line spare gang. I said to them, "If you want me you know where I am." So I went to my diesel loco on 'Sambo' yard and got on with the shunting operations. At about 8.20am the head shunter came up to the engine, "A 'phone call from Loco Bert, they want you over there. Shut her down and leave her, we're just going to breakfast anyway." Within a few moments I was walking back to the running shed, feeling somewhat elated at the prospect of a steam trip. I saw the R/F, "718 Bert. On the corner of the shed, all ready, Alfie Sutton's your fireman, Stew Lane are sending a pilotman to Clapham for the Victoria bit". He went on, "Good job you were about as Dick Ellis hasn't signed for the road and there is no one here who has, so away you go." I made my way to No. 30718 and climbed aboard, and my heart sank. The footplate was not clean, the tender had been coaled with what appeared to be the dregs of the coal hopper, and the dust was everywhere. Nothing for it but to have a bit of a clean up. Fortunately, there was a good handbrush and this was soon in operation. Alfie came aboard bearing a can of brew which he put in the dish after wiping it out, "Nip up and see if the tank is full Alf," I said. He did so and I blew up the brake. "Water's O.K. Bert", he reported, so the handbrake was released and we were on our way, calling in at the stores back door for a couple of sponge cloths in order to make the footplate look more presentable. We went light engine to Clapham Junction via the Skew Arch and Nine Elms Goods, then down the Windsor through line. Our pilotman was waiting at the London end of the platform. He came on to the footplate while the signalman had set the road for the Ludgate Line, so there was no more shunting to and fro, which would have been the case if we had been turned on to the 'down' Windsor local line, or worse still, through West London Sidings.

I had managed to clean the gauge glasses and protectors and the water level could now be seen without peering at them. We were soon in Victoria and our pilotman said to Alfie, "The shunter will hook on mate, you are not at Waterloo now you know!" Once the train brake had been created I checked that the coach brake pistons were well down, proving the in-going loco at the head of the empty stock had not created more than 21in of vacuum. When we left Nine Elms there was a 'black pudding' in the firebox. My mate had given it a lift with the dart and it now showed some signs of burning through, but Welsh coal takes time to get alight, especially when it has been shovelled whole heartedly into the firebox. Far better to put on a little at a time and allow the coal to burn through before adding more. A few moments prior to starting time, a well known ex-Camden driver, Laurie Earl, now several years into retirement, came up to look at the engine. He looked us over, at the tenderful of 'Nine Elms anti-glow coal' and asked, "How far do you think you will get with that stuff you call coal?" I replied, "Eastleigh", but his rejoiner was, "You will never make it!" as he returned to his seat in the train.

Victoria was left, being given a good bank out by the other loco, up the 1 in 60 of Grosvenor Bank. The T9 did well and we soon arrived at Clapham Junction, a pause to let our pilotman off and now we were on our own – not a footplate inspector in sight. Progress to our first stop at Staines for water was as per the timing, but the boiler was showing signs of distress, down to 140psi from the rated 175, and about half a glass of water, so the time spent standing at Staines was helpful in restoring boiler pressure. I looked at the fire, it appeared dirty and the coal was not burning evenly. If the fire was in good condition at that point the safety valves would lift as soon as the injector was shut off, and without the aid of the blower! Tank filled, a green flag from the guard and we were on our way again, followed probably by curious gazes from passengers awaiting their train to London. A motorman came out from his breakfast in the room to witness the unaccustomed spectacle of a steam engine on a passenger train taking water! "Long time since I've seen that", he called as I opened the regulator. The steam reverser on the T9 was in good order and held up all right and she marched up round the curve of the platform end onto Staines river bridge very well, past the three level crossings and speed was increasing. Egham distant was 'off' and I pushed the regulator onto the big valve to get a run up the bank to Virginia Water and beyond. But, lo and behold, the signalman there had the Chertsey line distant 'off' – we were booked to go on the Reading road so prolonged whistling ensued. Three blasts at a time, one for a signal post, one for the Chertsey line and one, which we wanted for our road. I expect the signalman made a hurried perusal of his weekly notices, found our train and quickly replaced the signals, changed the points and pulled off the correct signals, but the damage had been done. Speed was reduced of necessity and it was a long uphill drag through Longcross Halt and Sunningdale to the summit at Drake and Mount with an ailing engine. A 'West Country' Pacific with 250psi would hardly have noticed the gradient with eight on, but with our mount it was a vastly different proposition. We were in a sorry plight when I was able to shut off and coast down the gradient to Ascot, 120psi and water down to less than an inch in the glass! "Come over here Alf and let me see what I can do with her", I said to my mate. We changed places and I started the driver's side injector to get a more healthy level of water in the boiler. "Let her run Alf until the train is on the branch", I instructed. I had checked my signals, all 'off'. I reached for the pricker and gave the fire a good pull through and 'rux up', the blower was hard on and the boiler was slowly making steam. With 140psi on the clock, I turned off both injectors and blower and counselled my mate to, "Go for her". As we had now negotiated Ascot and were on the branch, the gradient was falling towards Bagshot and Alf adjusted the cut-off to 25 per cent and pushed the regulator right over. No. 30718 responded, the fire was hot and I fed the small coal evenly over the top of the half door, and the steam gauge was coming round so I started the injector. Another round was spread on the fire, and as I put each half shovelful on, the chimney blackened momentarily, indicating the coal had gone on to incandescent fire.

The T9 fairly swooped through Bagshot and was halfway up the succeeding gradient, which was not too long, but steep in railway terms, to the summit tunnel. After that it was a coasting session down the 1 in 60 through Camberley and Frimley to the junction. The safety valves were blowing and the gauge glass registered the water about an inch down the glass, just about the limit for a T9. I called my mate over to take the shovel again as I wanted to drive the engine over the junction on to the main line as I had never been over that short stretch. On to the 'down' local line we went, then turned out at Farnborough starting signals onto the main line and at that moment I estimated the 10.30am Waterloo to Bournemouth express, would be coming through Brookwood. It was not long before the boiler began to wilt, despite Alfie's efforts with the shovel and pricker. The further we went the worse the situation became, and at Hook the pressure was down to 110 psi with the water playing 'bobby bingo' in the bottom nut. Alf said, "Perhaps we can have a little 'shut-off' at the brickfields" – a short section with the gradient in our favour, between Hook and Basingstoke. I did shut the regulator for a short time, but it was hopeless as the fire was rapidly beginning to look like red hot sand in the firebox and we were travelling very slowly, at least for a passenger train. However, the brake was being held off, and obviously the vacuum ejector cones and the brake gear on the loco and train were in good condition. I have always thought it best to keep moving if possible, rather than stop for 20/30 minutes to 'blow up'. Often one is in the same sort of misery after ten or so miles, so, soldier on, through Basingstoke up to Worting Junction. There was no need to look early for the Bournemouth line signal at our rate of progress. All stop signals were 'off' and steam pressure hovered around the 100psi mark, and when she had 'made a bit' Alfie started the injector. Happily that was in good order as sometimes they are difficult to start when moving with low steam pressure, plus the fact that the water feed had to be manipulated by one's feet! So we crept on and at last we entered Roundwood Tunnel at the summit of the long bank down to Eastleigh. As we emerged into daylight, I closed the regulator, put the reverser into fore gear and let her run on the falling gradient. When I shut off, the water level dropped down out of sight, causing my mate to say, "It was there a moment ago". I countered with, "Is the injector working alright?" Alf looked over the side towards the smokebox as the injectors were placed just behind the leading driving wheels. "Yes, fine" he answered. It seemed a long time before the water came into sight, but it did and when we had two inches in the glass I suggested, "Turn it off Alfie and let's have some more steam." By this time we were through Wallers Ash Tunnel and I had half expected to be put into the Goods Loop at Weston box to let the 10.30am go by us and then out again on to the main line at Wallers Ash, but we were allowed to keep going. At Winchester I was able to give the old T9 some regulator and gained a little speed. At Shawford we were put on to the relief line for the last lap into Eastleigh and before we got to Allbrook the 10.30am roared by, driver Charlie Letchford shaking his fist in our direction. We must have 'caned' him for 25 to 30 minutes and even Charlie would not be able to recoup much of that before he arrived at Bournemouth. We were relieved in the Portsmouth Loop at Eastleigh by a set of that depot's men who were booked to take the train on at a later time to somewhere on the GW. I told them of our tribulations with No. 30718 and in their limited 'loco requirement' time they would not be able to give the engine a good square up, which was sorely needed. A grapevine report indicated that the old girl had stalled completely across a junction on the GW! – something which did not enhance the reputation of Southern engines and men! It was a shame that the engine was not 'stopped' at Nine Elms a day prior to the tour and the firebox and tubes given a good clean out so that plenty of steam would be forthcoming, then at least the T9 may have lived up to former glories under the name of "Greyhounds"!

Mallard on the Southern

Towards the end of January 1963, whilst awaiting our train at Salisbury, I was looking through the current issue of the *Railway Magazine* when I noticed in the section of advertised forthcoming special trains that the LCGB had requested that an A4 Pacific head a train out of Waterloo to Exeter at around 9am on Sunday 23rd February. I invariably knew my roster for a few weeks ahead and did a rapid calculation. We were 7am 'spare' on that day, and I remarked to my mate, Bob Payne, "There's an A4 coming over to work a special to Exeter on Sunday 23rd February and I reckon we'll get that job." He answered, "The Top Link will get that, we don't stand a chance." It was obvious that Bob considered the event to be a prestige one and would be automatically allocated to No. 1 Link. There was a rostered '8.00 spare' in there, also there was an agreement that Nos 1 and 2 links were of equal seniority in that where special or ordinary main line work needed to be covered by 'spare men', then the nearest man to any particular job would be booked in time order. I estimated that the turn would be shown as around 7.20am for 8.25am off the shed after preparing the engine, and as such we would be nearer the signing on time than the 8am men.

On the Monday morning prior to the Sunday, the Chief Roster Clerk, Doug Bridger, wanted to see me. He came straight to the point, "There's an A4 coming over for a special next Sunday Bert, I expect you know about it?" I affirmed I did. He went on, "Looks like you'll get that job unless anything else crops up and pulls you forward to an earlier turn." I fervently hoped that such a calamity would not occur and said so to Doug. He knew that all right and expressed the hope that nothing else would turn up. The next thing to arrange through our 'Guvnor', Mr Gilchrist, was for a shunter to be on hand at around 8.45am at Waterloo to couple the A4 to the train, as their tenders were fitted with an automatic coupling and as such were the domain of the shunting staff. Ordinary screw couplings and it was the loco fireman who 'tied on'.

On Saturday 22nd February, Bob and I were 2am spare and when we walked to the shed I saw a gleaming engine in No. 4 road. It was an A4 and closer inspection revealed it was the most famous one of all – *Mallard*! I saw the R/F on duty, Len Trigg, "I'm going to have a look around the A4 Len". He disappeared into the Roster Clerk's office and returned, "Here's the keys Bert, bring them back when you've finished." I thought 'that's a good sign, tool boxes locked up.' I was fully prepared to have a clean up on the footplate and had obtained some sponge cloths and a torch lamp from the stores. When I climbed aboard the sight of the footplate nearly took my breath away. It was spotless and the brasswork had been *scoured*, the gauge glasses were *clean*, showing about two-thirds glass of water, the fire had been dropped and very little steam showed on the gauge. A glance into the firebox revealed that it was commendably clean, whilst the oil lockers and tool boxes on the footplate had been wiped clean and kitted out with new tools etc. In the corridor on the tender was a set of overalls and a dust coat, along with two firing shovels, one short and one long handled for use when firing the back corners. I went underneath. Only two corks to remove and fill the oil wells, big end and small end – no valve gear to attend to as on the re-built Bulleids because of the 2 to 1 gear to operate the middle valve. What a pleasure it was to see an 'underneath' that had been cleaned, and it was not all 'top show'! The side rods and valve gear had been burnished, along with the buffers and front coupling.

Mallard surely was a sight for sore eyes, and all credit must go to the staff at Top Shed for showing the flag in no uncertain manner. I was confident it would be a case of 'handsome is as handsome does' and I looked forward to the following day with renewed interest and quiet excitement. Doug Bridger had booked Bob and I on at 7am for 8.20am off the shed, and after the necessary formalities I made my way to the A4 closely followed by my mate. There was a figure working on the outside of the engine. This was Frank Knight, a King's Cross Inspector whom I had met when I had had a trip on 'The Elizabethan' in 1956 with Ted Hailstone. He greeted me, "You got this job Bert?" I nodded and asked, "How far are you going with us Frank, and what are you doing with that oil feeder?" "I'm only going to Waterloo but I wish I was going with you. I will if George Harland doesn't show up, but he'll be there. I've oiled her so there's no need to worry about that." At that moment I did not know whether to be pleased or disappointed, I wanted to be able to say that I had oiled an A4 but there it was, the job was done and I did not propose to do it again after Frank had performed, after all, he was far more familiar with the class than I. To my surprise a wagon of hard Yorkshire coal had been placed alongside *Mallard* and a couple of shed chaps were waiting to *hand coal* her. It was obvious that someone in authority did not wish for the tender to be topped up with our Nine Elms soft coal and possibly cause steaming difficulties. The A4s were drafted to burn good quality hard coal, essential for the London to Edinburgh non-stops, so, no chances were taken.

As I had had several trips on the 'Blue uns' I was able to give Bob some advice on the preparation of the fire. As the chaps heaved lumps aboard, Bob put them in the back corners of the firebox, but he looked with some disgust at the small bladed shovels provided and attempted to use one of our Lucas shovels, only to find he could not turn the coal into the back corners under the baffle plate, so that was discarded. I then demonstrated the way to use the long handled shovel, dipping it under the baffle plate (also known as the flame scoop) and turning the coal into the desired spot with a one-handed movement. The vacuum brake was tried, along with the injectors, the coal watering hose working off the live steam injector on the driver's side. Coaling up completed, we moved out to top up the tender tank, then up to Waterloo. Our train was in No. 11 platform and Shunter, Charlie Mortlock, was waiting to couple us on. I stopped short of the train, Charlie made the necessary adjustments to the buckeyes then stepped out and 'called' me back. A thump as the buckeyes met, I reversed the engine and made the 'pull away test'. The pin had dropped and all was well, the shunter went in between again and put up the steam heat and vacuum pipes. The relieving Inspector, George Harland, was there and pronounced, "all together driver" as he came on to the footplate. Introductions were made all round and George asked, "Been on these before Bert?" "Yes" I replied, "But my mate hasn't. I've given him a few tips, back corners well up, thin across the front and no more than two-thirds of a glass of water etc.," The King's Cross Inspector nodded approvingly and now attention was directed to a fourth man on the footplate, Mr Earle Edwards, a railway officer who produced the necessary document permitting him to ride on the footplate. I had known him in 1948 but regrettably was unable to devote much attention to him due to the business of making sure everything was in order on *Mallard* at starting time, and Frank Knight had reluctantly departed.

Quite a few feet of film had been expended by the time the guard waved his green flag. I put the reverser down to 45 per cent cut-off (about 65 per cent in full gear) and opened the regulator. There did not seem to be the same amount of 'feel' in it as on the MNs but she moved the 11-coach train all right, assisted by the engine at the rear. Two or three turns of the driving wheels and I called to Bob to close the cylinder drain cocks, the lever on the fireman's side of the footplate. *Mallard* had started away without a slip but on Westminster Bridge she did a small one as I widened on the regulator. Hastily corrected, the cut-off was adjusted to 30 per cent and the regulator opened more. The A4 began to dig in and I managed to settle down, cut-off was further reduced at Vauxhall and I began to sense that this Top Shed engine was in good condition and willing to run.

One of the quirks of running society specials was that in addition to using unusual engines they also liked to run over roads where there was not a passenger service, so we were booked down the Windsor side out of Waterloo and over the East Putney line, re-joining the main line at Wimbledon. The 20mph turnout at Point Pleasant Junction was observed, and I had 'dropped' the lever out to 35 per cent to get us up the short sharp rise to East Putney and I thought to myself, 'she's going up here alright'. Then I noticed the reverser was slowly going forward; I had not put the catch in properly! – small wonder she was helping herself. Up to that point I had not heard the Gresley 'beat' the Kylchap blast pipe was not noisy and thereafter the engine ran quietly. Once on the main line, *Mallard's* true place, speed began to mount. I experimented with the reverser and regulator, and she needed plenty of regulator and short cut-off to get her along. I gradually pulled her up to 10 per cent cut-off and she just sailed along. The A4 was still pulling the train, without hesitation and without the feeling that the tender was going faster than the engine! A 'Merchant Navy' in 10 per cent cut-off would be almost 'blind' with all sorts of protesting noises emanating from the front end, but then, in full gear the cut-off was 75 per cent as against 65 per cent on an A4. No. 60022 was riding beautifully. I had set the reverser at 15 to 17 per cent as I feared the big ends may run warm on a too-short cut-off and anyway, the train had to be timed on a fairly fast timing. Approaching Byfleet, the vacuum ejector note changed. Bob had allowed the water to creep up the glass to just over three-quarters, so I called to him to shut off the exhaust injector, at the same time easing the regulator until the level of water had fallen. I opened up again when the priming possibility had been passed and the Gresley Pacific was soon into her stride again. Cecil J. Allen was riding in the train and he wrote in his *Trains Illustrated* report that, "The engine was unaccountably eased at Byfleet"!

At Farnborough I called to George Harland to sit in my seat and watch the road whilst I did a spell of firing this superb loco. It was sheer pleasure to do so. I hasten to add that Bob was not in any sort of difficulty but if he was reluctant to hand over the 'blade' he did not show it. Back

B.R. 29105

9.5 a.m TRAIN FROM Waterloo .... TO Exeter Ctrl ON Sun. DAY THE 24 OF February 1963

| | | Engine No. 60022 349 | From Waterloo | To Salisbury |

Name of Driver: Hooker, Jen. Payne
Stationed at: Nine Elms

Heat lbs.	Stations, Junctions, or District Boundaries	Timekeeping		Minutes lost					Minutes gained		Load		General remarks as to cause of delay and location. Formation of train, including alteration to load during journey
		Booked a.m	Actual a.m	Mins. Late Dep.	At Sta-tions	By En-gine	By Sig-nals	By P.W. checks	By other causes	At Sta-tions	By En-gine	Vehicles	Tons	
	Waterloo	9.5	9.5									10	357	
	Clapham Jn	9/12	9/14				2							Engine Clapham Jn
	Point Pleasant	9/15	9/17½				½							
	East Putney	9/17	9/19								½			
	Wimbledon	9/24	9/25½								½			
	Hampton Court Jn	9/32	9/33								½			
	Woking Jn	9/42	9/43											
	Worting Jn	10/5	10/7½					1½						PWC Winchfield
	Salisbury	10.35	10.36								1½			Max speed 95 MPH nr Crookwood

Exceptional occurrences, deficiencies in lighting, heating, accommodation and cleanliness of stock.

H.O. Inch & Harland, Kings X on engine

Weather: Fair. Some drizzle

corners were kept well up, fire thin and 'dancing' on the bars across the front of the grate, water level two-thirds of a glass and the pressure gauge showing just over 240psi. I saw all the signals in between bouts of firing and approaching Basingstoke, George was instructed to 'ease her down' for observance of the 60mph permanent speed restriction through the station. Once through there the regulator was pulled wide open again and at Worting Junction I handed the shovel back to my mate, donned my serge jacket again and took over the regulator. Halfway between Oakley and Overton the gradient changes to favour the engine and *Mallard* began to get a move on. At the Andover distant signal George asked me, "What's your road speed Bert?" I answered, "85" but he went on, "She's doing 93." I countered, "That clock's (speedometer) wrong", at the same time easing the regulator, but it wasn't, it was accurate and if the King's Cross Inspector had not mentioned speed we would have swept through Andover at 95mph.

The next section, Redpost Junction, George tried the water gauge on the tender, and learnt we had used about 3,000 gallons. I said, "That's fine George, we would have used around that amount on a fast train". The summit at Grately was surmounted in good style, another little joyful sprint through Porton, then speed was reduced to 50mph for the curves approaching Tunnel Junction, then to 10mph for the permanent restriction from Salisbury East box to the West box. Because of the longer LNER tender I went a little beyond the MN stop mark for water, which proved just right. The pipe was put in and my mate took charge of that. We were relieved by Bill Branscombe and his mate. Bill asked, "What we got here then?" I replied, "She's a good 'un, half a glass of water, pull her up and give her the regulator, she'll fly." Acknowledgement was given and somewhat reluctantly, we watched the A4 leave on her way to Exeter. Small wonder that the A4s were first choice for the East coast top jobs!

The 'Solway Ranger'

During 1963 there was a spate of Bulleid Pacific's being used for society tours away from the Southern and manned by crews unfamiliar with them, sometimes with unhappy results, such as running out of coal, or losing time to say the least. The Leeds Branch of the RCTS were planning an ambitious tour in June 1964 hoping to use a MN manned by a Southern crew and to aid them with their project the Secretary, Jack Smith, wrote to Mr R. H. N. Hardy, then at Liverpool Street, asking him to whom they should write with such a request. Within a few days, they received the reply, "Write to Mr Stanley Downes, M.P. Officer, Worple Road, Wimbledon, etc., and ask for Driver Hooker of Nine Elms"! That missive began a series of negotiated agreements with the motive power depots that would be affected, i.e. any crews who would have handled the engine would be compensated for any financial loss. Then there also was the business of obtaining the 'blessing' of my own colleagues at Nine Elms that my fireman, Ken Seaby, and I should be booked on the job, bearing in mind that we would leave Nine Elms on a Friday morning and return Sunday evening! A 'signing off' job that definitely was not on the regular roster. The OK was finally given, but even so, one man wanted an exercise carried out to the effect that the nearest man to three consecutive 10 o'clock turns on that particular weekend should be approached to determine if he was prepared to travel North. In the event, three men were sorted out amongst Nos 1 and 2 links, Fred Prickett, 'Conker' Gee and myself. The two former drivers named were adamant that they would not agree to go on the special working, which left me, so everyone was satisfied and the job was to be mine. Needless to say I was delighted and looked forward to doing it.

The next thing to be done was to select a 'Merchant Navy'. Whilst they were all all right, some were in better condition than others! I went to see Jim Cook, the Leading Fitter and outlined the situation, and he was all for selecting the best loco available. I asked the whereabouts of No. 35020 *Bibby Line* only to be told that she was on the 'stopped' list for No. 6 exams on the dates when we would be going to Leeds. Jim suggested No. 35012 *United States Lines* as she was the last MN to have a heavy repair and was due a washout on the day prior to the first leg. The decision was made, Jim made a note of it and I went about my normal duties. I was 'spare' along with my mate Ken when No. 35012 dropped in off the 'up' 'A.C.E.' to be squared up ready for boiler wash-out the following day. I asked the R/F if we could do the disposing work and, most important, book any necessary running repairs. "I was about to give you the job Bert, anyway. I know you'll be taking her away on Friday, so do your thing", that worthy replied.

As we walked out to the MN I noticed the left side safety valve was blowing slightly, and the gauge on the footplate registered 235 psi, so that was a job to be booked. A thorough driver's examination of the engine was made and any work requiring attention was noted, sanding gear, glands, ejector and injector cones, brakes, etc. After Ken had dropped the fire, the firebar condition was checked. I knew the firebox would be thoroughly serviced by the 'Ginger Pole' during wash-out, and checked for leaks by Jack Finch, the Leading Boilersmith. I saw Jim book during the wash-out day and he informed me that the work that was booked had been completed, the safety valve had been changed and the engine was booked for a steam test during the night (to ascertain if the safety valve lifted at the correct pressure, the usual practice). On Friday morning 12th June 1964, Ken and I booked on at Nine Elms at about 10.00 to go light engine to Leeds Holbeck, with a pilotman from Kew East Junction, on to the Midland main line at Cricklewood.

We were soon out into the country with sections governed by signalmen in their boxes pulling levers to operate the semaphore signals. At several of the sections the distant signal was at caution, causing us to slow down in order to spot the home signal which, when cleared the signalman then came out on to the veranda and photographed the MN as it went by. I was driven to ask the pilotman if the LM Region issued cameras to their signalmen! There was a change of pilotman at Leicester and eventually arrival at Neville Hill motive power depot was recorded. As our eight-hour day was up the R/F on duty said he would send out a pair of men to relieve us. I was pleased, but indicated that I would hang about to give any needed advice on our loco. The foreman appreciated that, and then our relieving fireman appeared, a big chap, who looked like a weightlifter. After the niceties, he asked, "Where does the bar go?" I lifted up the steel cover over the firebar rocking apparatus whereupon the rocking bar was inserted in its slot, a mighty heave and all the left side firebars came out of their sockets. I groaned, "That's torn it, its a boilermaker's job to replace those." There was now the onerous business of getting the fire and clinker broken up as it had to be pushed down through the displaced bars and into the pit. The other side was done more methodically, clinker darted and broken up and which then slid out easily into the hoppers and then the pit. Once in the shed, the boiler was filled and everything shut down awaiting the night boilermaker who came on duty at 22.00.

There had been a contingent of RCTS men hovering around whilst this drama was taking place and once *United States Lines* had been berthed, Ken and I were escorted to the 'lodge' near to the depot for a hurried wash. We were then whisked away by car to Leeds Great Northern Hotel, where a pre-tour meeting of the West Riding Branch was being held. Beer and sandwiches were given to us which proved most acceptable, after which, I was called upon to make a short speech. The main point of which, I stressed was that I hoped to prove on the morrow that Crewe and Doncaster were not the only places that could build Pacifics! The meeting over we were taken back to the depot, where the RCTS chaps were on first name terms with the R/F on duty, who assured me the firebars had been replaced. The MN was lit up and as we were on duty at 07.45 the following morning, he confirmed he would have her prepared for us. After a night of fitful sleep, Ken and I were at the depot in good time, the engine had been prepared and all that was needed now was a top up with coal and water, our pilotman arranging the necessary moves. Some hard coal was taken and I remarked to Ken that it would go through her like brown paper and all the scenery he would see would be floorboards and the firehole when she was opened up! We left the depot and we journeyed to some carriage sidings to couple on to our train, and formalities completed, progress was made to our departure point, Leeds City. The MN had, to my surprise, been cleaned during the night. The gangway framing was clean enough to kneel upon, – it was a long time since I had been able to do that! So far we had not seen a locomotive inspector, so when our pilotman was approached to allow an RCTS man aboard, this was agreed after a short consultation. Oddly enough, the thought of footplate inspectors had not crossed my mind until then.

We got the right away at the correct time, 08.43, on one yellow on the platform starter. I anticipated the next signal would be at least a quarter of a mile away, but in fact it was about half that distance and as it was showing red I needed to make a hurried brake application to avoid running by, the least desirable thing so far from home. Normal progress was made once we were clear of the environs of Leeds and a call was made at Hellifield to take water, after which the pilot driver was invited to drive *United States Lines* to Carnforth. There, a move that seemed somewhat complicated to me was made so as to get us the right way round to go to Grayrigg and Shap Summit. It involved attaching another loco on to the rear of the train, which dragged us around a triangle.

We had a change of pilotman for the run over the old LNWR main line and I asked him if there were any temporary speed restrictions on the way to Penrith and if the AWS was fitted and in working order. He answered, "No" to the first question and "Yes" to the second. The train 'grapevine' indicated that we were to go in front of the 'Birmingham' – with advice not to delay him! So, when we started off I did so with unusual vigour on my part, and good progress was made up to Grayrigg. Ken was busy with the shovel, the injector sang its song and the magnificent Bulleid boiler was responding well. The speed through Tebay was nearly 80mph, a good start for Shap incline, up past Scout Green, the engine speedometer showed 64mph and I was beginning to advance the cut-off a nick at a time in order to avoid a too-rapid fall off in speed. The boiler pressure was just under blowing off point and the water was well up the glass, all the ingredients necessary to turn the summit at a good speed. I was hoping this to be in the high fifties, but it was not to be as the pilotman called out "Shap Wells is 'on' mate". I had no recourse but to ease the regulator right down until about 60psi showed on the steam chest gauge, the gradient of 1 in 75 slowed the train adequately until it was necessary to apply the brake to stop at the obstinate colour light. It cleared and now we had to restart on the gradient. I think the MN slipped once, but the train was on the move again and all thoughts of a good speed over the summit had disappointedly gone. It seems a freight train was setting back into some sidings at the top of the bank, out of our way!

No point now in extending the engine too much, and once over the summit the speed rose quickly on the 1 in 125 falling gradient. Penrith was soon reached and we came to a stand, the MN was uncoupled from the train and an LMS Class 4 0-6-0 tender engine, running tender first, was attached to the front of the No. 35012 for the light engine run to Carlisle Kingmoor Loco.

In the meantime, a cardboard box filled with sandwiches and cans of liquid refreshment had come aboard, courtesy of the organising committee, and most welcome. Penrith was left and we ambled along at about 30 mph, the driver on the 0-6-0 making motions to me to hurry up. I opened the regulator a bit more and soon we were doing 60 mph – probably an unaccustomed speed for the freight engine! I gathered the other crew were in a hurry to get finished, after all it was Saturday lunchtime. Conditions on their engine must have been most uncomfortable, but if they could not stick it the driver could have applied the brake, but he did not until he had to, on the approach to Carlisle. We went through the station to Kingmoor and once in the depot he stalked off without a backward glance at us on *United States Lines*! As soon as the MN was over a pit Ken cleaned the fire and ashpan. I oiled all the 'pegwork' as I went around examining the engine. Thinking back to 1948, when I fired *Yeovil* over the Highland Line I remarked to Ken, "We won't take any of their coal, we'll shovel some forward, it will be better for you than their poor stuff." These chores completed, we signed off and for the first and only time in my life, and Ken must have been the same, we took 'short rest', a wash in the lodge then to a lounge wherein were some comfortable armchairs, and to my delight I dropped off for a couple of hours. Ken slept all right also, but then he could probably go to sleep on a clothes line!

We awoke somewhat refreshed, made a brew and ate the inevitable sandwich, then went to our engine to finish the preparation. Our fresh pilotman arrived, a Leeds Holbeck man who had come north 'on the cushions'. I had the mechanical lubricators to attend to and he volunteered to go to the stores to refill our oil bottles. Ken had turned the fire over onto the bare firebars and prepared the fire with some of the Welsh coal we had brought forward. The water in the tender was about 6in down and our pilotman said we could top it up at Citadel station, but the signalmen there put us anywhere except under a water column. I little knew then how close we were to come to disaster later on in the trip.

The tour train arrived with the Caledonian Single, No. 123, and Great North of Scotland 4-4-0 No. 49, double-heading. They were uncoupled and went to the depot, we then dropped back on with our 'Merchant Navy', Ken 'tied on', the brake was created and tested and we were soon on our way over what was a completely new railway to me. Once clear of Carlisle the MN began to run, until we were cautioned approaching Calgaith. (Rumour has indicated that a signalman there would keep his distant signal at caution under a small bribe from a photographer, so that a more dramatic photograph could be obtained when the driver 'opened up' to get into speed again.) After the slight delay *United States Lines* was put to it again, fulfilling my promise to Ken that all he would see would be 'floorboards and firehole'! For the climb up to Ais Gill I put her on 25 per cent cut-off and opened the regulator wide, the $17^1/_2$ miles from Appleby to the summit taking about $17^1/_2$ minutes at an average of almost 60 mph. On this stretch alone the MN had cut the timing by $12^1/_2$ minutes, albeit with only 310 tons.

Once over Ais Gill the gradient was in our favour, apart from one or two minor changes, and I rapidly needed to ease the regulator after Blea Moor Tunnel until only 40/50 psi showed on the steam chest gauge. Even so, No. 35012 was soon galloping along in the eighties, Ken had maintained a good fire, but as I was unfamiliar with the road I was unable to

LONDON MIDLAND REGION
(Midland Lines)

S P E C I A L   N O T I C E   NO. 693

FRIDAY, 12TH JUNE.

ON00 - LE Nine Elms M.P.D. to Holbeck M.P.D. ("Merchant Navy" Pacific locomotive)

Nine Elms M.P.D.		dep	10/30am	Wellingborough	pass	1.55pm
New Kew Jn.		arr	11*10	Kettering	pass	2. 8
– do –		dep	11*12	Desborough Nth.	pass	2.22
Kew East Jn.		pass	11.14	Market Harborough	pass	2.30
South Acton		pass	11.17	Kibworth Nth.	pass	2.44
Acton Wells Jn.	GL	pass	11X23	Wigston North Jn.	pass	2.56
DuddingHill Jn.		pass	11.33	Leicester	arr	3W 2
Brent Jn. No.2		arr	11L38	– do –	dep	3W10
– do –		dep	11L40	Syston	pass	3.20
Hendon		pass	11.46	Loughborough	pass	3.36
Silkstream Jn.	SL	pass	11X49	Trent	pass	3.54
St.Albans		pass	12.14pm	Trowell	pass	4. 4
Luton		pass	12.33	Pye Bridge	pass	4.20
Kempston Rd.	FL	pass	1X13	Morton	pass	4.30
Bedford Nth.		arr	1W17	Clay Cross	pass	4.36
– do –		dep	1W25	Chesterfield	pass	4.43
Sharnbrook Summ.		pass	1.44	*Rotherham Masbro*	arr	5W12
					dep	5.20

Southern Region (Nine Elms M.P.D.) P. throughout. Return 0000 Special 14th June.
Cricklewood M.P.D. Arrange conductor driver New Kew Junction to Leicester. Return
     home as passenger or as required.
Leicester M.P.D. Arrange conductor driver Leicester to Holbeck M.P.D. Return home
     as passenger or as required.   *Aydwarth* 5/53
                                                      Holbeck 6/139

- 2 -

NO.693 (Continued)

SUNDAY, 14TH JUNE.

0000 - Light Engine Holbeck Loco to Nine Elms.   *Holbeck 9/0*
     (S.R. Merchant Navy Pacific Loco).   *Aydworth 9/46*
                                                   Rotherham Masbro ar 10 W17
                                                   dep 10.23.
                                                   Beighton Jn 10/38

Chesterfield Mid		pass	10.53am	Kettering	pass	2. 0pm
Clay Cross		pass	11. 0	Wellingborough	pass	2.13
Morton Sdgs		pass	11. 7	Sharnbrook Summit	pass	2.24
Pye Bridge		pass	11.20	Bedford	SL arr	2W44
Trowell		pass	11.35	–do–	dep	2W52
Trent		pass	11.47	Flitwick	pass	3.14
Hathern	GL	pass	11X57	Luton	pass	3.34
Loughborough		pass	12. 4pm	St.Albans	pass	3.54
Syston North		pass	12.20	Napsbury	FL pass	3X57
Bell Lane		arr	12W30	Hendon	pass	4.16
–do–		dep	12L38	Welsh Harp Jn.	GL pass	4X19
Leicester		pass	12.41	Brent Jn. No.2	arr	4L23
Wigston South Jn.	ML	pass	12X51	–do–	dep	4*32
Kibworth North		pass	1. 3	Dudding Hill Jn.	pass	4.37
Market Harborough		pass	1.17	Acton Wells Jn.	ML pass	4X47
Little Bowden Jn.	GL	pass	1X20	South Acton	pass	4.52
Desborough North		arr	1*32	Kew East Jn.	pass	4.55
–do–	ML	dep	1X46			

Southern Region (Nine Elms M.P.D.) P. throughout. Off ON00 Special 12th June.
North Eastern Region (Holbeck M.P.D.) arrange conductor driver Holbeck M.P.D. to
     Bell Lane. Return home as passenger or as required.
Cricklewood M.P.D. arrange conductor driver. Travel as passenger per 9.50am
     St.Pancras to Leicester and conduct Southern Region men Leicester Bell Lane to
     Kew East Jn.

advise him in good time where to ease up on the shovelling. Consequently, there was plenty of fire in the box when we were going downhill and Ken kept the injector on to prevent wasting steam at the safety valves, so the water crept up and up well out of sight. Then, approaching Settle Junction the injector blew off, the tender tank was empty! For the first and only time in my life I was at a stand on a main line with an empty tank and the engine blowing off with a good fire in the firebox. That boiler though, had enough water in it to safely 'carry' us for 15 or so miles on level track. The Junction signals cleared and we were on our way to Hellifield, three miles away, and its most necessary water column. What a delightful noise that water made as it gushed into the empty tender and the relief I experienced then must have been plain for all to see.

The hard running and excitement of the trip was now over, with more sedate running now, on the remainder of the journey into Leeds. There a fresh pilotman climbed aboard for the empty stock run to the berthing sidings, which was soon completed, as was the return to Leeds Holbeck depot where we were relieved by a disposal crew. Both Ken and I were weary, so a bath and bed were the immediate priorities.

The following morning we made our way down into the Loco to pre-pare No. 35012 for the trip home to Nine Elms. Our pilotman came aboard, a main line man and a most pleasant and interesting chap. He told me he 'signed the road' from St Pancras to Glasgow! I experienced a slight pang of envy, but upon reflection, I too signed for nearly 400 route miles, but in a more congested area! On our journey south I was amazed at the number of coal trains standing on the relief roads awaiting their engines to begin work on the following Monday morning at 00.05 hours, or shortly after! A change of pilotman at Leicester where the ten-der tank was topped up, and then good progress was made to Kew East. Our new pilot driver stayed aboard to Clapham Junction on my advice, thence by train to Waterloo and the LTE service to St Pancras for his train home to Leicester. Our day was up when we arrived in Nine Elms Loco and we left *United States Lines* under the column. There was no doubt about the fact that the MN had performed well and had satisfied a host of RCTS members during her trip 'up north', fully vindicating the Society's request that the engine be manned by a Southern crew.

A Record-breaking Run to Salisbury
At the end of the 1964 summer service, the famous 'A.C.E.' ceased to run, following instructions from Paddington, as the line west of Salisbury was by then 'Western' territory. The former Southern West of England services were reduced to main line stopping trains and the lines west of Worting Junction were no longer maintained to their former high degree, when the Bulleid Pacifics could, and would, reach speeds in perfect safety above 85mph speed ceiling. So when on 16th October 1966, a high speed train was arranged in aid of the Woking Homes, fast from Waterloo to Salisbury, I hoped to get booked on the turn. My rostered duty was a two

way Bournemouth job so I approached our Roster Clerk, George Rowe with my problem. "Leave it to me Bert, no sweat as you're giving away five hours mileage money!" The daily alteration sheet was posted and I saw that I was booked on the special and my mate of the day was 'Rocker' Dedman. My own mate, Alan Newman, was on his rostered Bournemouth with presumably, the driver who would have had the special. But I was happy as I knew this would be the *last time* that I would ever work a fast train to Salisbury. The MN we were allocated was No. 35023 *Holland-Afrika Line* and 'Rocker' and I went about the usual chores of locomotive preparation. All was well until we arrived under the hopper to take coal, the tender was 'spotted' correctly under the chute, the coalman operated the long handle, 'black diamonds' cascaded into the near empty coal space and quickly filled up, but the coal kept coming as the coalman was unable to stop the supply. No. 35023 was rapidly disappearing under a mountain of coal! There was only one thing to do. I quickly put her into back gear, created a brake, checked there was not an engine right behind us, opened the regulator and slid backwards on to the pit, hoping that not too much coal would enter the smokebox via the wide chimney! As we moved away the coalman managed to close the coal chute, and doubtless a few well-chosen words helped there, but now we had to clear the excess fuel. The boiler was full of steam and water so I asked my mate to go and get the blowdown man to blow half a glass of water away. The injector could be started and the boiler pressure reduced, thus I was able to climb up onto the flat firebox top and clear the coal away from there and from the cab roof. 'Rocker' trimmed the coal bunker, the surplus going over the side as it was way up and would not pass under a loading gauge. The R/F came out to ascertain why we were late leaving the shed. He soon saw our plight and sent a fireman out to help brush off the gangways and tender top. The foreman had obviously had a word with the signalman in Loco Junction box because we actually left Loco and started our train in *nine* minutes. It was a situation which I heartily disliked, i.e., dropping back on to our train at almost starting time, especially with this special train.

Arthur Jupp, our Loco Inspector, climbed on, followed by the Tour Organiser – Derek Winkworth and the author of several railway books. Hurried introductions were made, I appraised Arthur of the coal hopper incident and also mentioned that I was going to 'let my hair down a bit' today, to which the reply was, "I'll put a cloth over the speedometer Bert!"

According to one writer, a 'copy book' exit was made from Waterloo, no slipping and steady progress over the maze of pointwork, but once beyond the advance starter No. 35023 began to speed up. The timing to pass Clapham Junction was seven minutes, but I was almost inevitably, near eight than seven, despite having only eight coaches in tow. I always disliked 'opening up' too quickly as this was likely to pull the fire into holes and give the fireman little chance to settle down. Provided the next timing point, Hampton Court Junction, was passed on time, i.e. normally 18 minutes, all would be well. I know some chaps would get by Clapham

```
15 October 1966
9.10 a.m. special train from Waterloo.

35023 (Holland-Afrika Line, without nameplates)
8 corr., 260 T. tare, 275 T. full.
Dvr. A.E. Hooker, Fireman Dedman (Nine Elms).
```

Miles.		Sched. (mins.)	Actual (mins. secs.)		Speeds (m.p.h.)	
–	Waterloo (d.)	–	0	00	–	
3.90	Clapham Junc.	7	7	42	54/40*	
7.20	Wimbledon		11	41	56	
9.75	Malden		14	10	68	
12.05	Surbiton		16	09	71	
13.35	Hampton Ct. Junc.	17	17	13	75	
17.10	Walton		20	08	80	
19.10	Weybridge		21	42	82	
	Byfleet and New Haw				85	
21.65	West Byfleet		24	17	14*	p.w. (long
24.30	Woking		30	47	–	
24.80	Woking Junc.	28	31	15	60	
28.00	Brookwood		34	11	67	
31.00	MP 31		36	47	73½	
33.25	Farnborough		38	32	80	
36.50	Fleet		40	55	84	
39.85	Winchfield		43	18	82	
42.20	Hook		45	45	18*	p.w.
47.80	Basingstoke		52.10		66	
50.30	Worting Junc.	50	54	25	72	
52.40	Oakley		56	06	78	
55.60	Overton		58	25	85	
59.20	Whitchurch		60	51	89	
61.10	Hurstbourne		62	08	93	
66.35	Andover		65	23	100	
72.75	Grateley		69	38	82 min.	
78.25	Porton		73	28	99 max.	
82.60	Tunnel Junc.	75½	76	37	–	**
83.70	Salisbury (a.)	78	79	43	–	

```
*  Speed restriction      **   very slow approach.
      Equivalent unchecked time 72 mins. or less.
```

Junction in the allotted seven minutes with a heavy train, but at what cost? – a fire torn to pieces and the fireman working frantically to get his fire right and restore his boiler water level somewhere near normal, all for the sake of a minute which could be recovered by Hampton Court Junction. But to get back to No. 35023. On this occasion our timing by the last mentioned junction was 17 minutes, only just slightly exceeded, but our speed was increasing to a maximum of 85 mph at Weybridge without the engine being pressed. Then came a long P.W. slack of 15 mph at Byfleet, duly observed, and once clear of this hindrance the MN was put to it again. A clear road through Woking was given and the speed rose up the 1 in 250 gradient through Brookwood to milepost 31 at the top, passed at 74 mph. I eased the regulator on the approach to Canal Bridge on a slightly falling gradient, then level through Farnborough where speed was 80 mph. It was 85 at Fleet and Winchfield but then came another cruel P.W. slack at Hook, 20 mph this time but not for too long. This 'shut off' enabled my mate to rally the boiler to around 240 psi so I was able to give *Holland-Afrika Line* some more 'stick' to get the train into speed again. Cut-off was 50 per cent as we came off the slack, gradually reducing as the speed increased; 25 per cent at Basingstoke, and the speed there was 65 mph, exactly as the permanent speed book indicated. There was no restriction round the curve at Worting Junction, but a year or two later a permanent one was imposed of 60 mph, probably due to falling track standards. Because of the two temporary speed orders we were just over four minutes late by Worting, but now the MN really began to run. Oakley at 78 mph, Overton 85, now on falling gradients, Whitchurch at 89 mph.

A mile or two back the injector normally used began to give trouble so the 'front one' was started, but now there was no means of laying the dust and there was plenty of it at high speed! We had to grin and bear it. Speed was still rising; 93 at Hurstbourne, and up the mile of rising gradient after Hurstbourne I widened on the regulator a little, then eased it over the top. All eyes now to spot the Andover outer distant, "It's off" from 'Rocker', and as we swept through Andover the magic 100 was reached and slightly exceeded. The faster the engine went the more smoothly she rode, the running surely was effortless. I was really enjoying the speed, indeed the whole occasion. I was not watching the speedometer, being far more concerned at looking for signals and where we were going. Up the gradient to Grateley I opened the regulator wide for the first time on the trip, and turned the top of the gradient at 82 mph. The regulator was eased again but the speed increased until we touched 99 at Porton. The water in the glass was below half and I remember thinking that if Porton or Tunnel Junction distant was at caution, there would be a heavy brake application, causing the water to disappear out of the gauge glass. However, we had the road and needed to brake normally to observe the 50 mph permanent speed restriction around the Laverstock curves to Tunnel Junction. At that time, there was a restriction to *10 mph* from Salisbury East Box to West Box and that is *slow*, and not always observed meticulously.

The special was routed into the old GW platform as it was going on to Taunton and I was unfamiliar with the correct place to stop, but it was managed all right. The usual flurry of activity then commenced, taking water, coal brought forward etc. I picked up the oil feeder to put a drop into the links and glands, and both outside big ends were *very warm*. I was unable to feel the middle one but as the 'stink bomb' had not gone off, it was all right. Despite the high speeds we were still just over a minute late arriving at Salisbury. However, the enthusiasts riding in the train were highly delighted and I was satisfied, as was my mate and our footplate guests – if you can call an Inspector a guest! Arthur Jupp and I were cleaning together at New Cross Gate, both went to Nine Elms on the same vacancy sheet, but when we went driving Arthur preferred to go on the supervisory path – I was more content on the footplate.

One of the passengers wrote to me and quoted that the time of 20 minutes and 12 seconds taken to cover the 30 miles from milepost 51 to 81, on average almost 90 mph was the fastest recorded. I guess it may have been bettered by Charlie Letchford or one of the other hard runners – but we shall never know! It all goes to prove just what magnificent engines Mr Bulleid's Pacifics were.

NINE ELMS MOTIVE POWER DEPOT

_____ DATE

NAME   HOOVER A E   PRESENT GRADE   DRIVER

REDUNDANCE NOTIFICATION

In consequence of the forthcoming closure of Nine Elms Motive Power Depot you will become redundant in your present grade as from the 10th July, 1967. This notification of redundancy is made now so that in accordance with the provisions of the Promotion Transfer and Redundancy for Footplate Staff, you may have the opportunity to indicate your willingness or otherwise to transfer within your grade to another depot within this Region.

I must, however, re-affirm the undertaking already given on the 18th February, 1965, that no member of the Footplate Staff will be discharged as a result of the Bournemouth Electrification and emphasise that this notification of redundancy is necessary to afford the facilities available to you under the Redundancy Arrangements.

You do not actually become redundant until July 10th, 1967, but in order to earmark staff for positions at Waterloo M.T. and thus expedite the training programme it will assist if you will reply by the 3rd December, 1966.

Until final diagrams are available it is not possible to give a final establishment for Waterloo M.T. Depot but the following are approxiamte requirements.

Driver   70
Firemen   30

It is also anticipated that approximately 6 Shunting Drivers positions will be required to be covered at Nine Elms.

For E. RICHARDSON

SHED MASTER

5

The 'New Beginning'

WHEN NINE ELMS finally closed on 9th July 1967, I must confess that I transferred to the Waterloo Mixed Traction Depot with a feeling that was something akin to relief. The dirt and slovenliness of the once Premier Depot of the Southern was now in the past. Just how some of the engines ran, and ran well, up to the last is beyond me, a fitting epitaph I guess to the robustness and reliability of the former prime mover. They had become unkempt, not entirely unloved, but almost crying out for some care and attention to be lavished upon them, if only to regain some measure of the pride and dignity of former years. The two 'Merchant Navys', Nos. 35028 *Clan Line* and 35008 *Orient Line* used on the 'Farewell to Steam' specials on Sunday, 2nd July, were kept in the shed for several days when every available man and boy, had a hand in the cleaning and preparation of the locomotives for the big day.

The MNs did well and I would have enjoyed being involved, but as my roster was to work the 1800 from Waterloo to Exeter (as far as Salisbury) with a 'Warship' diesel, any hope of securing a change-over was zero rated. Even if the drivers on the specials were 'Warship' trained, they could hardly be expected to accept a late turn for an early one, apart from possibly being in the limelight for a while. At least the two Bulleid Pacifics offered a glimpse of former glories, something to remember and who could have forseen the heights to which *Clan Line* would climb during the 1980s when tour trains were worked over various main lines. No. 35028 earnt an enviable reputation for cleanliness and reliability, and also proved popular with the BR crews who handled the strange locomotive (i.e. to them!). I shall never cease to be amazed at the dedication shown by the hard core of men and women of the Merchant Navy Locomotive Preservation Society (MNLPS) who work so hard to maintain the engine in such splendid condition.

No. 1 Mixed Traction Link
Transfer to Waterloo and entry into the No. 1 Mixed Traction Link went smoothly enough for me, along with other colleagues in the gang and there was still some traction knowledge to be gained. At first it was

pleasurable to go home comparatively clean, but after a turn on a diesel locomotive my wife began to complain of the odour which permeated my new uniform – Continental type, hat and all! She soon knew just what type of traction on which I had been working, as diesel fuel gave off its own unpleasant smell, apart from the exhaust fumes. I soon began to sigh for a sniff of good old coal smoke and oil passing through hot steam cylinders! On 19th July, nine days after the introduction of the new electric service to Bournemouth, a special train was organised to Southampton and return with about 350 people aboard. They had all had some dealings with the tremendous amount of work necessary when changing over to a new form of traction. The train provided was formed of a 4REP unit, No. 3005 and two TC units, a twelve-coach train. I was 'spare' on this day and was booked the job. I had no idea of the nature of the turn until Bill Neal, Chief Traction Inspector came aboard and outlined events. He warned me that there would be a constant procession of interested folk to have a quick look in the driving cab and the road ahead, and so it proved all the way to Southampton, completed in the 70-minute standard timing for fast trains. 'Change ends' was carried out in the 'up' siding, collecting a cup of coffee from the restaurant car as we went through. All the guests had a packed lunch and were obviously busy with that as the people who wanted to look in the driving cab were almost non-existent on the return trip, apart from Mr Gordon Nicholson. I was both surprised and pleased to see him as I did not recall meeting with him since the 1948 Loco Exchanges when he went to Scotland to ride behind WC No. 34004 *Yeovil*. He had a friend with him whom he introduced as the PR man of British European Airways. They remained in the cab from St Denys to Wimbledon and the outcome was that Bill and myself were offered a 'footplate trip' on an aeroplane! I thought to myself, 'That won't come off', but it did!

On 31st August, I was given leave and I had a letter from Worple Road, Wimbledon, (BRHQ) enclosing a first class pass to Gatwick, a complimentary airline ticket from Gatwick to Glasgow and return and instructions to meet the PR man and Bill Neal at the gate entrance to the Glasgow flight at 0800, if I remember correctly. We were soon on board, and the arrangements were that I would have the first leg in the cockpit whilst Bill would have the return trip to Gatwick. I was taken through by the PR man and introduced to the pilot and his co-pilot, sitting behind them on the left-hand side. Within a few moments we had taxied to the runway and were 'right away'. The acceleration was fierce and soon we were airborne. For the first time in my life a slight feeling of nausea was experienced when the aircraft, a BAC 111 jet, banked to put us on the correct course for Glasgow. I really enjoyed the flight, a marvellous new experience to see 'Newton's rings' on the clouds below us, the green fields of England and best of all, to see the *Q.E. 2* on the stocks, three weeks before she was launched on the River Clyde.

I had a new camera and it was put to good use. The air crew were excellent hosts, and it was probably unusual for them to have an engine driver in their domain. It had been mooted that they would ride with me on a Bournemouth train or on a Salisbury turn with a 'Warship' diesel, but to my disappointment it was not arranged and there was nothing I could do in the matter. Bill Neal enjoyed the return flight whilst I sat in the passenger compartment supping a welcome beer in the company of the PR official. All in all it was quite an unforgettable day.

One morning I was working the 05.47 to Bournemouth with a REP and two TC units, first stop Woking. After passing Surbiton, with the speed rising into the seventies, the air-brake went into emergency application. The train pipe needle on the brake gauge went from 70 psi to zero in what seemed record time, and the train came to a stand in rapid fashion, but surprisingly smoothly. I looked at the brake gauge, the main reservoir pressure was holding all right at around 100psi and I concluded that there was a burst train pipe somewhere on the train as that pipe reduction was too rapid for a communication cord pulling. I called the guard on the loudaphone, "You may have noticed we have come to a stand". I then went on, "I think we've got a burst train pipe, please walk towards me on the nearside and I'll walk towards you. Look for a burst pipe." Before I left the cab I applied the parking brake as the roller bearing vehicles soon began to roll on falling gradients. The guard had descended to the ground from the rear of the train and began to walk to the front, and as I walked back I peered at the brake pipes between the coaches. All were in order, but then the guard whistled and beckoned to me; he had located the problem. The train pipes had become uncoupled between the REP and the TC unit. I went in between, closed the cock above each pipe and reconnected them, and re-opened the cocks. I remarked to the guard, "We'll be alright now, I'll draw forward to Hampton Court Junction and tell the signalman what has happened." This accomplished we went on our way to Bournemouth, but instead of taking the train into the middle siding, leave it and then go into the room for breakfast, the R/F's instructions were, "Take it round to the West for examination". I was not exactly overjoyed but there it was. Examination proved that one of the brake blocks on the trailing bogie of the TC set had parted company with the hanger, and in passing had struck the train pipe, effectively uncoupling them, thus causing the rapid stop. One breathes a sigh under those conditions – now what? Instant possible remedies pass through the mind along with wondering what rule may have to be carried out.

I think the worst thing (apart from an accident) is when the platform starting signal is 'off', whistles are blowing along the length of the plat-form, one opens the controller and nothing happens! The instructor in the classroom says, "push up the windows, put your baccy on, get out your 'Faults and Failures' and check your procedures"! Not always easy as the thoughts of a 'Please explain' report loom large in one's mind's eye, but usually a press on the reset button, a 'change ends' switch not operated, or something equally simple, will provide the coveted amps gauge to move with power restored and the train moves. (Another little thing stored away for future use.)

The 'Warship' Diesel-hydraulics

I was trained on the Western Region D800 'Warship' class diesel hydraulics in July 1964, whilst in No. 2 Link as it had been considered that the drivers in No. 1 were too advanced in age to warrant the training. The majority did not wish it anyway as retirement was rapidly overtaking them, but there were several drivers within my own link of 1920 seniority. Dan Law, Jim Roberts and Frank Morris spring to mind, who accepted the change-over gracefully enough, being trained on the new traction by men young enough to be their sons! Gone was the concept that the older one was the more one knew – at least in some things. The drivers of my seniority seemed to absorb the diesels more readily, but we were only given the rudiments of operation, just enough for us to 'get by'. Management knew that the train running experience we had would serve us well on the diesels. We had a week in the classroom, a week on the track, running between Salisbury and Basingstoke with an empty stock train learning how to handle the stinking machines, a further week in the classroom for revision etc. After that we were deemed ready to take charge in service. I experienced some trepidation on the first trips, the two vacuum brake exhausters on the 'Warships' were notoriously slow, even with the 'speed up' button depressed. One could get the brake on all right but 'blowing it off' was an entirely different proposition. Extra care was therefore needed to stop the train at the correct place, particularly at Waterloo as the high nose of the 800s prevented a good view of the buffer stops. A marker post was subsequently erected in certain platforms to help the driver and avoid the stopping short problems and consequent operational difficulties, such as being unable to get a locomotive on to the rear end without 'tying up' other platforms.

On my third trip up from Salisbury on a 'Warship' the Exeter driver whom I relieved reported, "She don't half vibrate when you're in the high notches!" (Seven on the controller.) My heart sank; it all happens to me on Sunday evening! Anyway, we set off, all was fine up to the third notch, and at 20 mph the first gear change was made, (automatically). In the 4th notch vibration was evident and it became worse in the 5th and 6th. I was glad to close the controller at the top of the bank approaching Grateley and coast down into Andover. Restarting from there, the vibration seemed worse until about halfway between Whitchurch and Overton there was an almighty flash and a bang, the cab was filled with smoke and dust, and the front engine stopped. I looked at my mate, Bill Stanley through the gloom. He had risen from his chair and was about to open the cab door. "Where do you think you're going?" I asked. "I'm getting out of here" he replied. "Come back you fool" I said, "We're doing 60 mph". He then realised the position we were in – we were still going! – albeit on half power, and the smoke had cleared. "What now?", he asked. "I'll stop at Overton and look around, we don't need anything poking out to upset the third rail when we get to it", was my answer.

I duly stopped at Overton, with the 'Warship' off the shortish platform, and made my examination. Happily everything appeared in order, and the guard came up to ascertain the cause of the halt. I explained that we would be able to carry on with half power but would lose some time. Satisfied, he gave me a 'right away' and the 800 jerked into sluggish motion. A call at Basingstoke resulted in the Shedmaster at Southall, WR offering his help, which I was pleased to accept, thinking that he probably knew more about 'Warships' than I did. Nothing untoward happened on the remainder of the journey to Waterloo, where Charlie, the Charing Cross fitter was waiting. "What's gone wrong?", he questioned. "I've no idea. Something went bang and the front engine's stalled" I answered. "Start the front engine", instructed the fitter. I turned the engine start switch, a horrible jangling noise came from within the engine room, and I had turned the switch back almost before Charlie's "Whoa! The cardan shaft has gone. Do you think you can get her into the North Sidings?" He asked. "I got her from Overton, so I'm sure I can get her into the North Sidings!" I growled. The empty stock went off to Clapham Yard, No. D814 *Dragon* was berthed in the sidings, I entered the defect in the log book, went to the room, made out my 'ticket' and went home – somewhat thankfully I might add.

One evening, I was down with the 1900 from Waterloo to Salisbury, the date was 1st March 1965, motive power was 'Warship' diesel No. D815 *Druid*, and the night was cold, clear and very frosty. On boarding the engine at Waterloo I noticed the three fuel gauges were defective and a legend over the top proclaimed, "Fill to Spill", which meant that a full tank would be sufficient to work up from Exeter to Waterloo and return. It was common for the gauges to be defective so I was not unduly concerned, the engine was going well, the steam heat boiler was working to the maximum, but going up the bank to Grateley I felt a loss of power. I thought No. D815 was slipping on the frosty rails, then the front engine stopped, followed by the rear one. I said to my mate Ken Seaby, "Nip through to see if the boiler has shut down." He returned answering in the affirmative and I replied, "We're out of gas Ken. I wonder if she'll coast over the top and down into Salisbury". The vacuum brake was all right as the exhausters were running off the battery. However, it was not to be and the train came to a stand just short of Grateley inner home signal in uncanny silence. "What do we do now Bert?", asked my mate. "Nip back to see the guard Ken, tell him we are out of gas, but there's no need to protect in the rear as we are in station limits and we need to make arrangements for another loco", was my answer. After Ken had notified the guard, he was about to go forward to the signalman when I saw a light in the cess bobbing its way towards us. It was the signalman, riding on his bicycle "What's up driver?" he called out. "We are out of gas, I need an assisting engine to Salisbury and another to take the train

S. E. Area,
B.R.B.

DIESEL TRAINING PROGRAMME

Under the direction of the Railway Authority, we are entering into extensive training to modernise the traction thereon.

As a driver whose loyalty to the company is unquestionable we believe we may count on you as a patriot for full co-operation and we have therefore taken the liberty of training you for the 'Warship' Diesel.

Enclosed is a list of equipment necessary for each 'Warship' Trained Driver.

Please accept the thanks of the Railway Board for your co-operation in this enterprise, which we feel is so vital in the interest of all.

Yours faithfully,
W. E. Hope.
Chairman. B.R.B.

LIST OF NECESSARY EQUIPMENT FOR DRIVERS TO CARRY AFTER WARSHIP TRAINING PROGRAMME.

Equipment		Faults
1. Bottle of fuel	—	Fuel pump not running
2. Night light	—	Preheater not working
3. Set of darts	—	Puncturing E.A.B. valve
4. Packet of flints	—	Engine cranks but will not fire
5. Bicycle pump	—	Compressor failure
6. Packet of wet tissues	—	Testing vacuum leaks
7. Piece of rope	—	Transmission trips
8. Ice cubes	—	Cooling purposes
9. Sledge hammer	—	Tapping compressor governor
10. Block and tackle	—	Engine will not move
11. Bicycle bell	—	Fire alarm failure
12. No. 8. battery	—	Low batteries
12a Goldfish	—	Keep water circulating
13. Stirrup pump	—	Lub and water pump failure
14. Ship's anchor	—	Loss of air brake
15. Elastic band	—	Stop engine overspeed
16. Strong magnet	—	Changing directional gears
17. Spare hand	—	Holding reset button
18. Handle from fruit machine	—	Replacing dyno starter C.B.
19. Ejector seat	—	Engine beyond control
20. Sleeping bag – iron rations	—	Night out in wilds

IF ALL THESE FAULTS OCCUR AT ONCE, APPLY FOR
FREE PASS TO NEAREST ASYLUM.

to Exeter", I replied. "I'll see to it", that worthy went on, "It will be about an hour before help arrives".

We sat there, and it soon began to get chilly. I was turning events over in my mind and I thought about the 50-gallon emergency tank and resolved to try it. Out came the 'Faults and Failures' which directed me to the cocks which had to be closed and those opened, all in the engine room. That completed, I turned the front engine start switch, and the resulting uproar from the engine room and transmission alarmed me. I hurriedly returned the switch to 'off' and restored the cocks to their normal position. The assisting loco arrived from Salisbury, crossed over to the 'down' line and on to our 'Warship'. Ken coupled up and we suffered the indignity of being dragged to Salisbury. If No. D815 had managed to coast about a further mile and a half we would have been spared that as it is downhill from just west of Grateley to the Cathedral city. The dead loco was removed from the train and another 'Warship' hurriedly substituted to work forward. A few weeks later I was approached by a Salisbury driver who asked, "Are you the chap who ran out of gas at Grateley several weeks ago?" "Yes", I replied, and asked, "What have you got to tell me?" as he had the attitude of someone about to impart some important information. He continued, "Well, they towed the 'Warship' across to Westbury for examination, and a large cork was found in the fuel tank air vent. They concluded that a driver had been looking around the engine whilst fuel was being taken, had heard air coming from the air vent, thought it was a leak in the loco air brake system, so bunged a cork up the pipe!" So, whoever did that prevented the fuel tank being filled right up as air pressure built up until the pump stopped automatically, as it would normally do with a full tank. Defective fuel gauges were a common problem unfortunately, and in such cases there was no way one could tell how much fuel was available. If the fuel in the emergency tank was to be used then the change over from the main tank had to be made whilst the engines were running otherwise air locks occurred. The engines and transmission did not take kindly to being shut down suddenly and it all had to be done in the correct order. It would take around 20 seconds to run the seven notches back in sequence, so small wonder that I became alarmed when I attempted to restart D815 with everything out of phase!

The Class 47s on the Southern

Once a driver had been trained on the 'Cromptons' (Class 33s) a week's conversion course was considered sufficient to be able to take charge of the Class 47s, modified modifieds and all! Only a few drivers were so trained and I was in that group, not, I hasten to add because of any affinity towards diesel locomotives, it just happened. One of those drivers was one Phil Ginger who had a phenomenal knowledge of London's railways which stemmed from his steam footplate career at Willesden. Phil was a big man and most unfortunately the examining instructor had to fail him because he was unable to walk from one end of a Brush 47 to the other through the engine room. He was all right on a 33 as the diesel engine and internal equipment was much slimmer. It was one of the worst moments of the examiner's career to have to fail Phil for such a reason as he had grasped the fundamentals of diesel traction more readily than most of us in the class.

In the small group of Brush trained men was one other, George Lloyd I think, who signed for the Portsmouth road. During the holiday season I would look at the list of special trains booked to run from Willesden to Portsmouth on a summer Saturday or vice-versa and powered with a 47. I would be removed from my own rostered turn and be booked on the special because of route and traction knowledge. I did not lose in the monetary sense as I would be paid either for my own turn (mileage moneys) or the special, whichever was the higher. Sometimes I would get an earlier turn for a rostered late one or vice-versa again, but it all evened out in the finish.

The 47s were fast, powerful locos and one needed to be careful to regulate the speed to conform with the timetables then in use. Probably the most unsatisfactory episode relating to the class in the eyes of the railway enthusiast was on the day of the last 'Bournemouth Belle' working on Saturday 8th July 1967. The word had gone forth that the last 'Belle' was to be 'Merchant Navy' hauled, crewed by the senior Nine Elms driver, George Holloway and his rostered fireman. The train seats were all booked by enthusiasts eager for a final steam hauled train, but it was not to be. A 47 hauled the beautiful Pullman cars and a host of disappointed train enthusiasts asked for their money to be refunded! It would appear the SR authorities lost face on that occasion, much to the disgust of the would-be travellers.

Electro Diesels and 'Cromptons'
The EDLs (Electro Diesel Locomotives) required a three week training period in July 1966, all in readiness for the change-over the following July. They were grand little engines, 1,600 hp on electricity (3rd rail) and 650 hp on diesel. Oddly enough they would inch a freight train up a bank more easily on diesel power than with the shoes down and drawing current from the third rail. At low speeds under those circumstances the pyrotechnics reached alarming proportions, especially over small gaps in the third rail! The locos were air fitted for braking with adequate compressor capacity to feed an air fitted train. Also, they had vacuum brake exhausters for working vacuum fitted trains and in theory it would be possible to run a dual fitted train; a TC unit on the front of the EDL with vacuum fitted stock behind it. I do not think it was ever tried experimentally, the brakes would be created all right but whether or not the vacuum brake would go on when the brake was applied from the TC unit is a debatable point!

In the early days of the new traction I relieved a Bournemouth driver there. He drew up driving an EDL and behind that was a 33 diesel loco and two TC units, all air fitted. "Does it go?", I enquired. "Like a bomb" was the answer. It was true, the adequate power available gave me my fastest ever speed (up to that time), up through Micheldever, at just over 85 mph. I though I had better ease up as the speed limit on 'Cromptons' was 85 and I did not want the drama associated with a burst traction motor!

On one occasion, a Sunday evening, I was working an 'up' Salisbury train with a 33, and passing Walton-on-Thames, at just above 80 mph there was a loud bang from the engine room. I lost amps and the diesel engine reverted to idling, the brake was still all right so I let her coast. The speed was gradually falling the whole way to Waterloo until the train came to a stand on Westminster Bridge – so near and yet so far. I climbed down immediately, went to the nearest 'phone to speak to the signalman, "Is the pilot able to get on the front of the Salisbury and drag us in as I've lost amps", I asked. The signalman answered, "Yes driver, he's clear, I'll call the Yard Foreman to get him out". The crew were on the '350' Driver Stan Stonestreet was soon appraised of the situation, the signalman set the road, the ground signal was cleared and within a few moments the station pilot was on the front of my 33. The coupling was thrown over, the second man (I did not have a mate) regained his cab and Stan pulled my train into the designated platform. I stopped the train with my power brake, reset some circuit breakers in the engine room and regained power. An entry was made in the log book, and I learned subsequently that a flashover had occurred. The loco had been taken to Stewarts Lane for examination of the generator windings and until this had been completed train hauling was not permitted. The 33s had an 'overcharge button' in the cupboard under the driving desk, I think in the No. 2 end, and if the train pipe on the loco became over-charged above the 70 psi pressure, the engine brake and vacuum brake would drag on. Pressure on the button to release the overcharge would restore the brake to normal. I have noticed that when one is without a second man, and the overcharge is to be released, the button is invariably at the *other* end of the loco – necessitating a stop to adjust it.

When the HBs later (Class 74) came on the scene, there was another conversion course, and after the sophisticated control on the EDLs, 36 notches plus four stages of field weakening, the HB control was crude. There was nearly another 1,000 hp to deal with, yet the master controller only had four power notches, 'shunt', 'series', 'parallel' and 'weak field', with a switch to operate when running a freight train. Then a 'weak field' could be obtained in the 'series' position of the controller, which was most useful when working a van train or freight where speed had to be limited. I was working the Weymouth boat train one morning and the loco would not get into real speed, and I said to myself, "She's only going like a freight train!" This led me to think of the change-over switch, and sure enough, the switch was in the 'freight' position. The controller was closed, the switch operated and the controller re-opened to the wide position, and the HB leapt forward to full speed and I heaved a sigh of relief.

The riding qualities of the machines left a lot to be desired, and I would not have been surprised to learn that one had derailed itself. The 600 hp Paxman diesel engine, fitted therein when they were rebuilt from purely electric locomotives, was an extremely noisy affair, and one needed ear-plugs despite special bulkheads to keep the fearful noise out of the driving cabs. One peculiarity of the diesel engine was that its noisy note did not change from idling when a load was put upon it, such as lifting a 13-coach train out of Waterloo, it was advisable to have the diesel engine running at this stage because of the numerous gaps in the third rail, until the advance starter and West Crossings were passed. It was always a relief to shut down the diesel engine and get the shoes down, then carry on with electric power. They were very powerful locos, easily capable of reaching 100 plus mph so some driver revelled in this but the authorities stepped in, and a speed limiter was introduced. Then, as soon as the speedometer reached 91 mph the power was cut off, thus keeping to the line speed of 90 mph. When the speed fell slightly, the power was restored. For a while they worked the oddball loco hauled train, the 15.30 to Bournemouth, amongst the normal REP and TC units on that service. The return train was made up of vans, a job I liked on pleasant summer evenings, with the sun shining on one's back, a complete contrast to the 'down' journey when heading into the sun, which reflected off four or more running rails. I used to pull down the sun visor, hang a sheet of newspaper therefrom and place another piece across the bottom of the window and peer through a small-ish opening in an effort to reduce the glare on sunny days. If ever there was a need for tinted glass it was on the traction of that era.

A Return to Steam
After I had been at Waterloo in No. 1 Mixed Traction Link for about three years, had sampled every duty within the MT framework, (apart from the Waterloo & City), and far from enjoying more amenable times on duty, the situation became much worse in my opinion. Drivers and second men would be booked on duty during the small hours to perform menial work, perhaps lasting for a mere two to three hours, and no thought would be given by those responsible for producing the working diagrams as to how the men would get to work. Not everyone lived within walking distance of the depot. A time on duty of 00.05 to carry out some diagrams would be much more suitable for the vast majority of train crews. Turns such as the Bournemouth paper train were accepted around 02.00 as it was a running turn and mileage monies to come. Against this background I went home on one unforgettable morning, and after the greeting formalities, my wife Renée remarked, "You're getting more and more miserable and harder to live with. Get yourself a ruddy steam engine!" I perked up at this and thought that idea has possibilities. Where shall I get one? Where do I run it? I will have to join a club to get the use of a track. How much will one cost? That *is* important.

It seems as though fate stepped in at this juncture as Richard Hardy wrote to me asking if I would like to buy a 3½in gauge three-cylinder 4-6-2 locomotive and tender. "It's been standing in a garage for years, some of the time in an inch of water, but it is cheap" he wrote. I jumped at the offer and Richard in his capacity as Area Manager, Liverpool, made the arrangements to get the loco boxed up, sent by train to Euston where my friend Bob Jones and I met the train. We took charge of the boxes, afterwards delivering them to Bob's home in Westbourne Grove where a preliminary examination was made. It was quickly discovered a good deal of work needed to be undertaken. The regulator was seized, a bogie wheel had fallen off, the check valves were stuck on their seatings and worst of all the driving wheels would not revolve, lending substance to Richard's assertion that it had not been in steam for a considerable time! But, in the capable hands of Bob Jones the various defects were overcome, and oil in the right places produced freedom of movement, Locktite was used to 'glue' the bogie wheel back on its axle, the check valves were cleaned and safety valve springs and ball valves checked over and re-assembled. Hot water was put into the tender and freed the handpump non-return valve so water could be pumped into the boiler. The gauge glass was dismantled gently and the water ways poked through with softwire to ensure they were clear. The smokebox and firebox still had char and ash in them, indicating that the loco had not been 'put away' properly, anyway all the debris was removed and the smoketubes were brushed out. The firebars were hinged at the front and secured with a pin, and when removed the bars dropped down so that clinker etc. could be raked out into the ashpan opening. After this the bars were replaced and the ashpan dealt with, and in locoman's parlance "Given a good square up."

I must say that most of the foregoing was not a strange chore to me, except that previously I had only indulged in the scale of twelve inches to the foot locomotives! Came the great day when we took the 4-6-2 to the track of Bob's club near Hampton Court Junction signal box. I think it was a Thursday as that was Bob's day off from his business. He brought along a car battery operated blower to raise steam and as the engine had a double chimney one orifice needed to be blanked off with a small coin to make the blower effective. Charcoal soaked in methylated spirit made a good 'bottom' on the grate, burning readily, to which small coal, about the size of a thimble was added, four or five 'teaspoonfuls' at a time until a good fire was burning. Steam began to rise and when about 20 psi showed on the clock the electric blower was disconnected and removed. The coin, now quite hot, was removed and loco's own blower was applied, steam pressure rising steadily, one of the safety valves lifting at 60 psi so Bob screwed it down a little at a time until another 20 psi was showing on the gauge. The tender hand pump put water in the boiler, albeit a little slowly, but the real test was to come. In the absence of an injector would the axle pump deliver water into the boiler? Because of his experience of small locomotives, Bob drove the 4-6-2 around the Malden Club track a couple of times. He stopped and was using the hand pump, "Axle pump's not too good" he remarked. "Won't maintain the boiler. You have a go now Bert." I clambered onto the driving trolley, checked the boiler and fire, added some coal, pumped more water into the boiler, eased off the blower and gently opened the regulator. It started like a true three-cylinder Pacific – it wanted to slip as it began to move – a feeling I shall never forget, driving one's own engine for the first time! Speed picked up quickly, I adjusted the cut-off until she 'kicked' then let it out slightly. Up the rising section of the elevated track the loco sailed, on the down gradient the regulator was eased right back, blower on as the blast on the fire had gone. Bob was correct, the axle pump was not able to maintain the boiler so the test run was brought to an early close!

Eventually, with the help of other model engineers, an injector was fitted, although it never worked satisfactorily. The axle pump was overhauled but in reality one with a larger bore would have eased the water feed problem. If the pump was flooding the boiler the by-pass could be adjusted to reduce the feed. A model steam locomotive follows the full size ones in every respect, and it needs an excellent boiler with good firing to make the water climb in the gauge glass and yet maintain the steam pressure close to the red line. On a model, everything happens much more quickly than on full size – steam and water can disappear in a 100 yards of running! The smaller the loco the sooner one is in trouble – from Gauge 1 (1³/₄in) to the true narrow gauge engines of 2ft gauge. I am always reminded of the story of the main line driver who wanted the boiler water maintained at one inch down the gauge glass and the needle on the red line! His young fireman of the day retorted, "Make up your mind. Do you want steam or water, you can't have both!"

The First Trip to Canada
In September 1971, the BR Staff Association at Euston organised a charter flight to Toronto. This was open to BR staff in the London area, and the period in Canada was to be three weeks. My wife Renée, who had a fear of flying, suddenly decided to go on the trip, so I hurriedly wrote off to the secretary and obtained two seats on the '707'. As soon as confirmation was received I contacted my friend George Barlow, foreman driver on the 15in gauge Romney, Hythe & Dymchurch Railway. "Do you know anyone who works on the Canadian Railways George?" His answer was in the affirmative, "There was a chap here from Montreal a few years ago, name of Jack Hewitson, he works on the CPR, I'll give you his address." Thus another pleasant chapter opened in our lives. . .

I wrote to Jack and had a reply within a week (about twice the speed of today's postal service!) which resulted in being invited to spend a weekend at the home of one of Jack's friends in Peterborough, Ontario, one Henry Moxon who had a 3¹/₂in gauge elevated track in the garden. Renée and I were to catch a morning train from Guildwood to Peterborough where Henry and Jack met us. My sister drove us to

Guildwood to catch the train and as we sat in it awaiting departure I saw her conversing with the conductor and once the train was on the move he came to us and asked, "Have you got your transportation?" I was non-plussed for a moment, then realised he wished to see our tickets! They were in order, the conductor went on, "I guess you would like a trip up front, we'll go see the Engineer at the next station. I'll keep an eye on your good lady." Sure enough we went forward to see the driver on the diesel locomotive, and the second man was looking out. The conductor called up to speak to the Engineer and he came across the footplate and opened the door. The conductor went on, "This chap belongs to a railway club and would like a ride". The Engineer looked askance at me, I could see he was about to refuse, so I hurriedly spoke up, "I'm a driver from the Southern in England." "That's different" he remarked, "climb aboard the flamin' locomotive!" So there it was, our first trip on a Canadian main line train and my first, and entirely unexpected, experience on the footplate. The driver must have had good seniority whilst his mate looked as though he was nearly 40. We chatted, and he told me that due to a reduction in train services, promotion was slow, and I sympathised with the former steam loco fireman. They were pleasant hosts and I enjoyed the trip to Peterborough. A loco man is a loco man the world over and I am proud to have belonged to such a unique body of men.

On arrival at Peterborough it almost seemed as though Jack Hewitson expected me to arrive on the locomotive as he, and Henry Moxon were awaiting at the spot where the engine would stop. If Jack was surprised to see me climb down from the diesel cab he did not show it, and his approach was not unlike the well known one of the African explorer – "Bert Hooker I presume?" Introductions were quickly made, Renée was collected from the train and soon we were on our way to Henry's home. It proved to be a most enjoyable weekend. Jack had brought along his latest model – the '18' (he builds one every year, all $3^1/_2$in gauge). This was a freelance 2-4-2 tender engine with outside Stephenson gear, roller bearings and a Giesl ejector, the only one I've seen in $3^1/_2$in gauge. I drove this little loco around the track after I'd had a turn on Jack's 'Schools' class 4-4-0, which although only a two-cylinder loco the appearance was correct, and was numbered 940 and named *St Trinians*. Jack was to build a 'Super Schools' some years later, Belpaire firebox, three cylinders and valves actuated by a Gresley 2 to 1 motion; another very successful locomotive. I think my favourite one of the unique engines that came from his workshop was a German 4-6-2, deliberately made into a 4-4-2 to cut down the weight. This was a delightful silkily running engine I enjoyed driving on other visits in later years.

During correspondence the following year, 1972, I learned that Jack sold some of the locos he built and asked about the '18'. "Yes, you can buy it but how are you going to get it over from Montreal to England?" The problem was solved when Eric Smith, a pilot with British Airways and a friend of Bob Jones, volunteered to ferry it over when he had a Montreal flight, as part of the 'Pilot's baggage!' I was astounded at the simplicity of it all. I notified Jack of Eric's flight number and time of arrival and departure, they met at the airport, went to Jack's home in Verdun, had a meal and returned with the engine and tender, already boxed up separately for ease of handling. I had given Eric a cheque on my bank for the stipulated price, he in turn gave Jack a cheque on his International bank and everything worked smoothly. The '18' was delivered to the Malden track by Eric a few days later when I was most pleased to take charge of it. I've had many pleasant hours running it on my local club's track, the Welling & District Model Engineering Society, adjacent to Falconwood station S.R. At the time of writing it is in pieces due to a periodical boiler examination, which it passed, and by the time this appears in print the '18' now named *Jackson*, should be running again.

For Eric's kindness I was able to give him the odd trip to Salisbury on a 'Crompton' which he appeared to enjoy more than flying aeroplanes! I guess it is the difference that appeals.

Jack's engineering expertise is phenomenal, and he occasionally gets called upon by his former employers, the CPR to deal with steam engine work that sometimes crops up, whilst his knowledge and know-how in the $3^1/_2$in gauge is always in demand. At meetings where a number of engines are run I think he secretly hopes one will fail so that he can remedy the defect, as he appears to derive more pleasure mending than running them!

George Barlow

George Barlow, previously mentioned, is another man with a vast experience of small gauge locomotives, particularly from 15in gauge downwards to $2^1/_2$in, a locomotive historian of some ability and my friend since 1948. Through him, I met several people who had steam railways in their gardens and enjoyed the experience of driving small steam engines. One man I must mention is the late Bob Hobbs, who worked on the Romney, Hythe & Dymchurch Railway, running Captain Howey's favourite locomotive *Hurricane*, a 4-6-2. Bob kept her 'squeaky clean' and treated her so lightly she would barely steam! A true LSWR enthusiast, as soon as he saw a photograph of that company's locomotives he would utter a heartfelt "Cor!" Bob ran a $3^1/_2$in gauge railway, the Willow Tree Railway, in a caravan park near his home in Hythe, using his own locos, giving children rides for a small fare, the proceeds of which went to buy Guide Dogs for the Blind – nine in all. He had hoped to get a tenth, but unhappily, he died. The RH & DR ran a special train, hauled by *Hurricane* in Bob's memory, donating the monies raised for the tenth dog – a wonderful gesture.

Transfer to Slade Green and Retirement

During 1975, I had to move house to Slade Green and to avoid travelling to and fro to go on duty I made my last transfer to Slade Green depot, a mere five minutes walk from home. After a few months learning the road to cover all the turns at Slade Green I 'took' on, then for the last six years of my career I was an 'electric motorman'. Six marvellous years working with as good a bunch of railway men as one would find in the country – one large link that took two years to go around! The work was in total contrast to that at Waterloo. The earliest turn, as I recall was 03.30 'cover' and Tom Hazard loved that job. I very seldom had a duty before 06.00 as someone was always willing for the real early ones and I revelled in turns around 07.00 to 08.00, but oddly enough most drivers on my shift preferred to be finished around mid-day and I was happy to help them achieve that objective. All the work was suburban commuter and going to Slade Green was like a breath of fresh air. I must say that I felt generally better in health – no more diesels and none of the pressures associated with working on several different types of traction and braking systems. All EPB stock, but the route system was far more complicated than out of Waterloo. From New Cross into Charing Cross, Cannon Street and Holborn Viaduct was not to be undertaken lightly, it must have been a nightmare in steam days during foggy weather, running under semaphore signals. I mentally 'took my hat off' to the enginemen of the steam era prior to electrification and to the motormen of the pre-war Southern Railway, who ran a more intensive service with the early electric trains using pure Westinghouse brake – and the system ran like clockwork! In addition there was the fitting in of freight trains that ran from Hither Green to King's Cross etc., and to Plumstead via Dartford, where the engine had to run round its train to proceed up the North Kent line. *Railwaymen* ran the job in those days. My father saw it all from the footplate and motorman's cab whilst I had but a glimpse of it.

Since I retired in July 1981, I am pleased to say that I have not been bored for a moment. The occasional trip to a preserved railway enables one to get a sniff of coal smoke and warm oil – to wallow a little in nostalgia does a power of good. When I was invited to drive MN No. 35027 *Port Line* on the Bluebell Railway on her first revenue earning trip several years ago, the intervening twenty-odd years just slipped away as I sat on the familiar seat. It had been arranged that Stan Symes, retired driver from Bournemouth and currently active on the Swanage Railway, was to be my fireman on this momentous occasion. It was good to see a former colleague amongst other folk in the preservation movement. Even today, when I meet old mates and my former firemen, the talk is invariably about real 'prime movers', not about the modern locos, though they have their interest, and with the power generated they are not a challenge – unless it will not move! When I put a fire in my little 2-4-2 I always think of George Barlow's quote, "It's great to be able to boil a drop of water in the proper manner!"

The Running Shed Alphabet

A   stands for Axle, the thing that runs hot,
nobody oiled it, the Driver forgot.

B   the Boilerwasher, greasy, top-booted,
in water he works, and in time gets web-footed.

C   is for Coal, and when steam you are short of,
no finer excuse than 'bad coal' can be thought of.

D   is for De-railments, engines and trains,
they always occur in the night, when it rains!

E   is for Engines, we haven't sufficient, no never,
they go into shops and come out worse than ever.

F   stands for Fitters, the guardians of tyres,
there are some born mechanics and some are born liars.

G   the Goods, for which the engine you've just 'wangled'
after hours of deep thought you learn the train's
cancelled.

H   is the Hat, worn by the Loco Controller,
the man that's the boss is the one in the bowler.

I   the Inspector, who often pops in,
they're like Solomon's lilies, they toil not, nor spin.

J   is for Journal, a statement the driver supplies,
in some quarters known as 'a tissue of lies'.

K   for the Keep, of oil it holds plenty,
but when it's examined, is usually found empty!

L   for the List, that great cause of perpetual strife,
you put the thing up then run for your life.

M   for the Men, to please all is the thing,
the result makes one cry 'O death, where is thy sting'.

N   for the New engines we sometimes obtain
from the works for a month, then they go back again.

O   for the Office, the place you are usually not in,
there are Offices good and others darned rotten.

P   for the Pilots, for which the Traffic implore
they'd take your last engine, and still ask for more!

Q   is for the many Queer stories you're told,
how the crank pin ran hot or the firebox got cold.

R   means Running Foreman, driving's his hobby,
he'll shunt the whole coal road, with men in the lobby.

S   is for Steam, that was down below 'thirty'
explanation 'tubes leaking and fire very dirty'.

T   is for Test on which your report goes
but where it all leads to the Lord only knows.

U   refer to the Underneath, and a subject for jest as there is not one
cleaner who believes that an engine has got one.

V   is for the 'Schools' class, they came not to stay,
the Lord gave, and now He hath taken away.

W   is for Water, the boiler ran short of
when the lead plug went, the water was thought of.

X   is the Cross all Locomen carry
in trying to please every Tom, Dick and Harry.

Y   is the Youth that we sigh for in vain,
when we open the letter which starts 'Please explain'.

You may look through the Stores and all over the Shed
but you won't find a 'turn' that is covered by Z.